# Pruning
# Made
# Simple

# Pruning Made Simple

**WRITER**

Barbara Ferguson Stremple

**PHOTOGRAPHER**

Saxon Holt

**ILLUSTRATOR**

James Balkovek

LAWN & GARDEN

Product Manager: Cynthia Folland, NK Lawn & Garden Co.

Acquisition, Development and Production Services: BMR, Corte Madera, CA

Acquisition: Jack Jennings, Bob Dolezal

Series Concept: Bob Dolezal

Project Directors: Jane Ryan, Jill Fox

Developmental Editor: Janet Goldenberg

Horticultural Consultant: RG Turner Jr

Photographic Director: Saxon Holt

Art Director (cover): Karryll Nason

Art Director (interior): Brad Greene

Cover Design: Karen Emerson

Cover Photo: Saxon Holt

Interior Art: James Balkovek

Photo Assistant: Peggy Henry

Copy Editor: Barbara Chan

Proofreader: Fran Taylor

Typography and Page Layout: Barbara Gelfand

Indexer: Sylvia Coates

Color Separations: Prepress Assembly Incorporated

Printing and Binding: Pendell Printing Inc.

Production Management: Jane Ryan, Brad Greene

Cover: Deadheading spent flowers on a rhododendron lengthens its blooming season (see page 26).

93  94  95  96  10  9  8  7  6  5  4  3  2  1

First Edition

Library of Congress Cataloging-in-Publication Data:
Stremple, Barbara Ferguson.
    Pruning made simple / writer, Barbara Ferguson
    Stremple : photographer, Saxon Holt : illustrator, James
    Balkovek.
       p. cm.
    Includes index.
    ISBN 1-880281-14-7
    1. Pruning.  I. Title.
    SB125.S86  1994
    635.9' 1542 --dc20                                    93-20811
                                                              CIP

Special thanks to: Maile Arnold; Valerie Brown; Fleurette Evans; Goldbud Farms, Placerville, California; John's Rose Garden, Napa, California; Kozlowski Farms, Forestville, California; Sonoma Valley Waldorf School; Freeland and Sabrina Tanner; Paul Vossen, UC Agriculture Extension Agent, Sonoma, California.

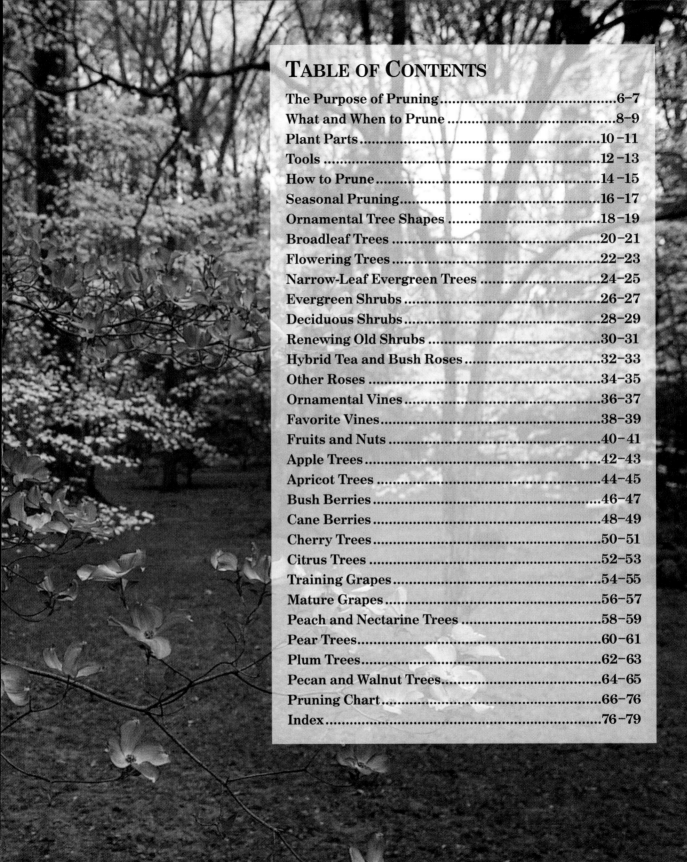

# TABLE OF CONTENTS

# THE PURPOSE OF PRUNING

## WHY PRUNE?

Whether you inherit a garden of mature plants or are installing a new landscape, there comes a time when the trees, shrubs and vines need some pruning. Perhaps they are new and need to be shaped, or maybe they've grown too big. Whatever the reason for needing to prune, you may feel perplexed about how to begin. You are not alone. Gardeners at all levels of expertise hesitate when the need for pruning arises.

Many people think that pruning is tricky and they may harm their plants. The truth is that if you follow some simple guidelines, pruning is a fairly easy task. While you may not do the job exactly right the first time, you will learn with practice. If you are like many gardeners, you will find that there is something surprisingly satisfying about the work itself.

Pruning should benefit the plant as well as the look of your garden. There are many reasons to prune: to control the size of a plant, to encourage new growth, to increase the number of flowers or fruits and to remove dead, diseased or damaged plant material.

A lot is said about the correct time to prune; however, timing is not always critical. If disease is present, prune immediately. If you plan to remove much of the plant, it is important to choose the correct season since timing is crucial to the plant's recovery. If you just need to do a little shaping, timing is less important. There is an old adage: "Prune whenever your knife is sharp."

Read the information presented in this book and learn the basics of where and how to prune. Then you can make your cuts with confidence.

# THE IMPORTANCE OF PRUNING YOUNG PLANTS

There are two good ways to avoid a lot of pruning. The first is to select plants that will grow no bigger than the space allotted them. The other is to begin pruning when plants are young, so that they'll grow to the size and shape you want them to. Prune before you have a problem and the job will be fairly simple—and a lot less work.

When you select a plant at the nursery, make sure to ask what its ultimate size will be. Tell the nursery staff where you will be planting it and ask their advice on its suitability to the space.

Many plants from the nursery need some trimming and shaping once you get them home. They may have been pruned tall and narrow or short and squat to fit in a nursery's storage space. Their limbs and roots may have been damaged during transit or may break as you set the plant in the ground. You'll need to cut off these misshapen or broken parts.

Once you have planted, cut off any broken limbs. You may find that your new tree or shrub has a branch growing toward a fence or wall, growing downward or angled too closely to the main trunk. If so, remove the branch right away. Waiting until it is larger means creating a big gap in the plant when you remove the limb. It also means leaving a large pruning wound, which takes longer to heal, allowing more time for diseases or insects to invade.

Any plant grown for its flowers or fruit has special pruning needs, whether it is a vine, shrub or tree. In addition to any pruning required after planting, many of these plants need some pruning every year to promote optimum flowering or fruiting. The first part of this book introduces basic pruning techniques. The second part has guidelines for pruning the most popular garden plants.

**CAUTION**

Removing very large limbs can be dangerous; hire a professional.

# WHAT AND WHEN TO PRUNE

## A SERIES OF QUESTIONS TO ASK

Often, the trick is just deciding whether something needs pruning. To get past this point, ask yourself about the plant. Is it new? Is it too big? Is it misshapen? Is it supposed to flower or fruit, but not much is happening? If you say yes to any of the above, you may need to get out some sharp shears and possibly a pruning saw.

So, what next? Just how do you go about the job? You must identify the plant so you can define the task. Is it a tree, a shrub, a vine? Is it *evergreen* or *deciduous* (loses its leaves seasonally)? If it produces flowers or fruits, when do these appear and where? On this year's growth? On last year's growth? Or on growth that is two or more years old?

To find the answers, look for your plant's name in the Pruning Chart beginning on page 66 and read the sections of the book that discuss it. If you don't know the name of your plant, ask a gardening professional to identify it or read the parts of this book that describe its general character.

Once you have answered these questions about your plants, you may determine that they are fine and don't need pruning. If the answers indicate pruning, study the techniques described on pages 10–11 and 14–15 and the instructions for your specific plant before you attempt the job.

The tree is deciduous and the branching is vigorous but too low to pass under comfortably. Remove the lower half of the fork in late winter.

These roses bloom once in summer. They need pruning in late winter.

## THE PRUNING PROCESS

Many gardeners hold off pruning a plant until it grows too large. At this point, they make the mistake of just whacking away at the plant until the size is right. Usually the result is not so attractive, and the plant often responds with loads of bushy, shapeless, weak new growth.

Pruning when the plant is young creates a stronger plant with superior flowers and fruits, and a size and shape suited to its place in the landscape.

If you have a new plant that is not yet in the ground, remove the container (if it has one) and trim all broken roots just above the break. After planting, cut off broken branches or those that look diseased. Then prune out limbs that cross or grow downward. Remove branches that deviate from the natural shape of the plant. If there are a few well-placed branches that are too long, cut these back to a bud facing in the direction you would like the plant to grow.

After this initial attention, the plant may grow well and need little pruning over the years. As time passes, ask yourself the questions on page 8. If you decide that some pruning is in order, always start by cutting out any dead or diseased wood. Then decide how you want to change the overall shape. To accomplish this, remove the largest branches first, stepping back between cuts to assess your work. Finish with smaller cuts to refine the plant's shape.

You can encourage new growth with light thinning or pinching, or decrease the size of your plant by heavy pruning.

The shrubs are overgrown. They are evergreen and need heading back in late spring.

# PLANT PARTS

If you know the anatomy of a plant, it is easier to prune correctly. Parts with black bars across them are undesirable; prune them off. When removing a twig, cut to a bud and make the cut close and at an angle. When removing a branch at the trunk or back to another branch, cut parallel to the remaining wood.

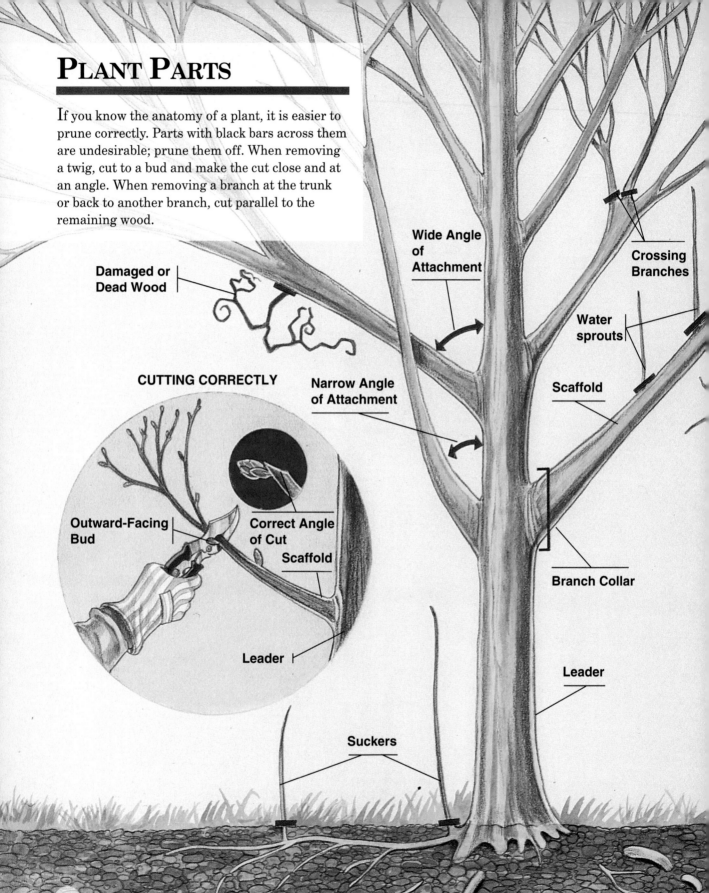

**Damaged or Dead Wood**

**Wide Angle of Attachment**

**Crossing Branches**

**Water sprouts**

**Scaffold**

**CUTTING CORRECTLY**

**Narrow Angle of Attachment**

**Outward-Facing Bud**

**Correct Angle of Cut**

**Scaffold**

**Branch Collar**

**Leader**

**Leader**

**Suckers**

10

Forks of
Equal
Size

Branch Growing
Down or Under

## PARTS OF A FRUITING BRANCH

Terminal Bud

Lateral Buds

Spur

Last
Year's
Growth

Bud Scar Rings

Year Before
Last Growth

# ANATOMY OF A TREE

The framework of any plant consists of a stem, side shoots and roots. On a tree, the main stem is the trunk (also called the *leader*). The side shoots are the branches or laterals and the largest of these are called *scaffolds*. Strong scaffold branches are those with angles of attachment that form wide V-shaped *crotches*. A narrow crotch means the branch is almost parallel to the trunk and can split off the tree easily in high winds or under heavy snow or ice. A wide crotch means the branch is more at right angles to the trunk, which results in a stronger attachment. The *branch collar* is the swelling at the trunk where the branch grows out. Never cut into this collar when you cut off a limb; the growth cells that heal a pruning cut are in this collar.

*Suckers* and *water sprouts* are fast-growing, upright shoots that emerge from branches, from the trunk or from shallow roots. They tend to be weak and undesirable.

*Buds* produce leaves or flowers. Narrow buds contain leaves, while plump buds produce flowers that will develop into fruit. The bud on the end of a branch, called a *terminal bud,* is *dominant:* it is the first and fastest to grow. *Lateral buds* are those on the sides of a branch. When you prune a branch, the last bud left becomes the terminal bud and is dominant.

On apples, apricots, pears and plums, the fruiting buds, which form flowers and then fruit, grow on very short, knobby branches called *spurs*. When you pick fruit from a spur, it is important to pick carefully so that the spur does not break off but remains in place for next year's crop.

*Bud scar rings* are lines around the branch that mark where a bud started growing in the spring. You can track each year's growth by counting bud scar rings from the tip of the branch back. If you count one ring, this means all the wood out to the tip is this year's growth. Each ring back along the branch marks a preceding year's growth.

# TOOLS

The most important attribute in a pruning tool is sharpness. A dull blade cuts poorly and the wound heals slowly, allowing pests or disease to attack. Also, good quality tools are a smart investment because they work easily, stay sharp longer and wear well. If you keep them clean and oil them occasionally, they will last a long time.

**PRUNING KNIFE** For smoothing large cuts. Requires some skill to use well.

**HEDGE SHEARS** For shaping and controlling the size of hedges.

**ANVIL HAND PRUNER** Blade cuts against a flat metal anvil, which may crush the shoot. Cannot cut as close as scissors-style. Best on green wood up to 1/2 in. thick.

**SCISSORS OR HOOK-AND-BLADE HAND PRUNER** Always cut with the blade closest to the trunk or to the part of the plant that will remain. Otherwise you will leave a stump.

**STRAIGHT SAW** Works well on large limbs but needs room to maneuver freely.

**BOW SAW** Strong and stable; cuts on both the forward and backward strokes, unlike the others. Won't work in tight spaces.

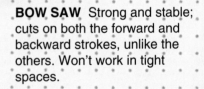

**CURVING SAW** Good for pruning large limbs. Can be folding or rigid handled. Folding type is easier to store, but the blade must be locked into place before cutting.

**ELECTRIC HEDGE SHEARS**
For large shearing jobs. Efficient, but makes it easy to cut too much.

**LOPPING SHEARS**
**Hook-and-blade or anvil style**
Long handled to be held with both hands so you have greater leverage and cutting power.

**WOOD RASP** For smoothing large cuts.

**CHAIN SAW** Use for very large limbs. Handle with care. Never use for overhead cuts. Get a professional for overhead work and large jobs.

**EXTENSION SAW** Allows you to remove small branches overhead.

**EXTENSION LOPPER** Allows you to cut back material that is out of reach. Do not use on large branches; the wood and material may fall on you.

13

# How to Prune

## Techniques

Gardeners often use these techniques in combination, but rarely use all on the same plant. When pruning, never remove more than a third of the foliage at once.

*Pinching,* using the thumb and index finger, removes soft, green shoots and directs growth to buds below the pinch, resulting in a fuller, bushier plant. It is the most basic form of pruning.

*Heading* reduces the size of woody plants. Trees or shrubs are often headed when they grow into utility wires or a structure. Unfortunately, heading destroys the plant's natural shape and encourages many buds to sprout below the cut, causing dense regrowth.

*Thinning* is a method of selectively removing branches to open up the plant's canopy while maintaining the plant's natural form. If a tree is too tall, it can be shortened by cutting back the main trunk to a strong lateral branch. This drastic thinning technique is known as *drop crotching.*

*Shearing* is like heading on a smaller scale. It is best applied to shrubs used as formal hedges or topiaries. Shearing changes the natural shape of the plant and must be repeated regularly.

*Pollarding* is a high-maintenance method of controlling the size of fast-growing trees. In winter, all the limbs are headed back to stubs; in spring, a flush of growth sprouts from these stubs. Over time, the stub ends enlarge and look gnarled. It is important to cut back to this enlargement (but not into it) each year. London plane trees, horse chestnuts and elms are the trees most often pollarded.

*Topiary* is a pruning art form in which artistic or whimsical shapes are created from plants that respond well to shearing. Good topiary plants are boxwood, hemlock and yew.

**Pruning Large Limbs**

**First**  Make a cut about 1 ft. from the trunk on the underside of the branch and about 1/3 of the way through the branch.

**Next**  The second cut from the top should be at least 6 in. beyond the first; cut down until the limb breaks off.

**Last**  The final cut should be as close to the trunk as possible without cutting into the branch collar (see pgs. 10–11).

# Pruning Techniques

**Pinching** With the thumb and index finger, nip off the tip of the branch or stem just above a bud or leaf.

**Shearing** Cut back all branch tips uniformly, creating a smooth, even surface. You may have to repeat several times during the growing season.

**Heading** Cut the branch back to a side branch or a bud; try to avoid leaving a stub.

**Pollarding** Cut developed 3–4-year-old scaffold branches back to 2–4 ft. stubs. Head back to stubs each year.

**Thinning** Remove the branch where it emerges from a larger limb, the trunk or the ground.

**Topiary** Shear plant to develop desired shape or form. Prune several times during each growing season.

# SEASONAL PRUNING

## Spring

Spring is a great season for removing damaged wood or suckers and for pinching out buds that are heading in the wrong direction. In most cases, you should avoid heavy spring pruning. The sap is moving in plants and too much pruning can cause profuse sap loss, or *bleeding,* in many of them.

A lot of spring growth is made by using up food stored in the plant from last year. If you prune in the late winter, the plant has not used up its stored food and can begin to grow from the pruning cuts using its stored reserve. A spring pruning cuts off new shoots that used the stored food for their growth. The plant then has to grow again using whatever food reserves are left or by photosynthesizing new food using the few leaves remaining on the plant after you pruned. For this reason, spring pruning has a greater dwarfing effect than pruning at other seasons.

Spring is the best time to shear evergreen hedges and rose hedges. They grow fastest at this time and need to be directed early.

## Summer

There are several pruning jobs best performed in summer. Prune spring-blooming plants in early summer, just as the flowers start to fade. These plants flower from buds that grew the previous summer and have been dormant all through the winter. In spring, the buds swell and bloom. If you prune in winter or spring, you remove the flower buds before they bloom. Deutzia, forsythia, honeysuckle, lilac, mahonia, rhododendrons and azaleas, certain spiraeas and weigela all bloom in the spring and should be pruned in early summer. The plant has plenty of time during the current summer to grow new wood and flower buds for next year.

Late summer is a good time to thin overgrown trees. Heavy summer pruning is more dwarfing to a plant than winter pruning, largely because you are cutting off leaves that would otherwise remain to make food for next spring's growth. If you are trying to tame a fast-growing plant, however, heavy summer pruning may be advisable.

Although it is best to prune most fruit trees in late winter, you can prune them in late summer. The risk of disease infestation at the pruning wound is greater at this time. If fire blight is a problem in your area, wait until winter to prune.

## Fall

Fall is a good time to prune if you live in a mild climate. If your winters are cold, be careful with pruning at this time of year. In cold climates, it is advisable to refrain from heavy pruning that encourages lots of new growth to sprout. With cold weather right around the corner, an early freeze can easily injure this tender growth.

In mild climates prune roses, clematis and woody vines in the fall rather than late winter. You can do some pruning to reduce the size of a tree or shrub, as long as you finish well before cold weather sets in. Also, prune out any mechanical injury to a tree such as broken limbs.

Fall is also the time to mark your deciduous trees and shrubs for winter dormant pruning. Using paint or plant ties, mark the branches that are sick or diseased. This helps you identify them in the winter when all the dormant, leafless branches look the same. In mild climates you can remove sick branches whenever you spot them.

## Winter

Winter is a great time for a number of pruning tasks. Fortunately, it is also the time when you are the least busy in the garden and can turn all your attention to the job.

In late winter before buds begin to swell, prune plants that bloom on new growth, such as abelia, heather and hydrangea. This way, the plant does not waste its energy on growth that might get cut off if you were to prune later, when it is developing flower buds. When you prune before spring growth occurs, you shape the plant first; flowers then develop on the new growth produced that year. Before you cut, confirm that the plant does not bloom on wood made the previous year. If it does, do not cut that wood.

Do all dormant pruning in winter when plants are not actively growing. Most plants have lost their leaves and the framework of the tree or shrub is easy to see. In very cold climates, pruning too early in winter may mean you need to prune again at the end of the season to cut out any winter injury that occurred late in the season. If you live in a cold-winter area, wait to do your dormant pruning until late winter when the coldest weather is past.

# ORNAMENTAL TREE SHAPES

If you know the natural shape of your tree, it is easier to decide which branches to prune. The following lists indicate mature tree shapes; keep in mind that these are generalizations.

## Rounded

| | |
|---|---|
| Acacia | Horse chestnut |
| Ash | Little-leaf linden |
| Basswood | Norway maple |
| Beech | Red maple |
| Callery pear | Saucer magnolia |
| Catalpa | Southern magnolia |
| Chinese pistache | Sugar maple |
| Crab apple | Silver maple |
| Goldenrain tree | Tulip tree |

## Columnar

| | |
|---|---|
| Canary Island pine | Irish yew |
| Columnar maples | Italian cypress |
| European hornbeam | Lombardy poplar |
| Incense cedar | Upright English oak |

## Open/Irregular

| | |
|---|---|
| Birch | Red oak |
| Cypress | Sassafras |
| Eucalyptus | Scarlet oak |
| Evergreen pear | Scotch pine |
| Ginkgo | Sycamore |
| Hackberry | Tea tree |
| Live oak | White oak |
| Olive | Valley oak |
| Poplar | |

## Weeping

Australian willow
California pepper tree
Camperdown elm
European white birch
Mayten tree
Norway spruce

Weeping higan cherry
Weeping mulberry
Weeping willow
There are also many
   weeping varieties of
   upright trees

## Pyramidal

American arborvitae
American holly
Austrian pine
Bald cypress
Bay laurel
Black gum (tupelo)
Cedar
Colorado blue spruce
Douglas fir
English holly
European hornbeam

False cypress
Fir
Hemlock
Larch
Pin oak
Redwood
Shortleaf pine
Spruce
Sweet gum
Western red cedar
Yew

## Horizontal/Spreading

Apple
Crab apple
Cork tree
Dogwood
Honey locust
Japanese maple

Japanese red pine
Japanese black pine
Live oak
Mugo pine
Redbud
Silk tree

## Vase

American elm
Autumn gold ginkgo
Crape myrtle

Pagoda tree
Service berry
Zelkova

# BROADLEAF TREES

## PRUNING BROADLEAF TREES

Most people think of broadleaf trees and deciduous trees as being the same, all losing their leaves in winter. Some broadleaf trees don't fit this pattern. Magnolia, holly and eucalyptus trees are all evergreen, although they have broad leaves. The broadleaf trees discussed here include both deciduous and evergreen types.

There are many reasons for having a broadleaf tree in your yard. They are beautiful—a vigorous, well-branched tree gives a home a solid, enduring look and sets off the color and design of the house. They give cool shade to relieve the home, the landscape and passersby in the hot days of summer. They screen unattractive views, decorate blank walls and fill in open spaces, adding to the beauty of the scene. As a result, reckless pruning can detract not only from the shapeliness of the tree but from the harmony of its surroundings.

Before you prune, find out all you can about the tree. If you do not know its name, take a small, leafy branch to your local nursery and have it identified. Then look for it among the trees listed on pages 18–19 to determine its natural shape. Finally, read the pruning guidelines for your tree in the Pruning Chart beginning on page 66.

Most broadleaf trees need relatively little pruning. Begin by removing broken or diseased branches and crossing limbs. It is also a good idea to cut back wayward branches that spoil an otherwise pleasing outline. Decide what the tree does for its location and prune with this, and the needs of the particular tree, in mind.

Trim back overlong branches to an outward-facing bud.

Branches should be evenly spaced around the trunk and up and down it.

If tree must be staked, be sure to use pliable material such as the plastic links shown here.

Make sure the tree has one strong leader with no competing side branches of equal height.

# SHAPING NEW TREES

Pruning a tree when it is young can make all the difference in its appearance and health as a full-grown landscape plant. It gives the tree a good shape right from the start, making subsequent pruning easier. Because the cuts on a young tree are relatively small, they heal more quickly than on an older tree, giving diseases less opportunity to attack.

Due to space constraints in commercial nurseries, many young trees have grown in crowded conditions that produce weak trunks in need of staking for the first year or two.

Once your tree is planted (and supported by two stakes and plant ties, if necessary) you need to assess its shape. Determine which branch is the leader and leave it alone. If there are several branches that could all be leaders, select the strongest straight branch and prune back the others to a side branch or outward-facing bud. Remember that new branches continue to form higher and higher as the tree grows taller, while those already on the trunk remain at their present height and just enlarge in diameter. Eventually you must remove branches too low to walk or sit under, unless the tree is intended as a climbing tree for children and you do not need to mow beneath it. Also remove branches that are heading toward the street, sidewalk or driveway, unless they are high enough to pass under. On young trees, these low branches should be headed back but not removed completely for the first few years. Their leaves produce food for the tree, help to shade the trunk and contribute to the growth of a strong trunk that is wide at the base and tapers slightly all the way to the top.

Whatever shape your tree is destined to take, your pruning goal is to establish a branching pattern with the main scaffold branches one to two feet apart and spaced evenly around the trunk, like a spiral staircase. This pattern allows the sun to reach the interior, and therefore more of the leaves, for optimum growth.

# FLOWERING TREES

Landscape trees that flower are a treasure during their blooming period. They light up the landscape with their color, and their falling petals are magical. Although they are not grown for edible fruit, many of these trees do set a crop that can be quite decorative.

*Magnolia soulangiana* is a deciduous tree known by the common names Saucer magnolia and Tulip tree.

## Encouraging Bloom

Prune flowering trees when young to promote a vigorous, well-branched form. Select a strong central leader and establish a good branching framework, removing suckers, crossed branches and any damaged or diseased wood. Unlike commercial fruit trees, which are heavily pruned to produce more or larger fruit, flowering ornamentals do not require extra pruning to force more blossoms to form.

To get the most enjoyment from blossoms, prune flowering trees after the blooms fade. Keep the trees open and well shaped so that light gets into the interior. Dense, overgrown trees usually bloom sparsely and only on the ends of branches.

Prune no more than one-third of a badly neglected tree each year, or you will weaken the tree. Even if the tree is heavily overgrown, it should take only two to three years of pruning to get the tree into shape. Just be sure to time the pruning so that you do not cut off all the flower buds.

If you are interested more in a good crop of decorative fruit, prune in late winter or you will drastically reduce the tree's production. Flowering crab apples are common ornamental trees that produce both flowers and decorative fruit. They are also rampant growers. They are easier to prune in winter, when leafless, but this encourages lots of dense spring growth which is not always desirable. You will, however, get more fruit following winter pruning. If your tree is blooming well, summer pruning will control the tree's size and density better.

If you want to cut blooming branches to bring indoors, wait until the tree has been blooming well for a year or two. Otherwise, your cuts will slow down the tree's growth.

# NARROW-LEAF EVERGREEN TREES

## SHAPING NARROW-LEAF EVERGREENS

Although a few evergreens have broad leaves, most have needles or very narrow, needlelike leaves. Common narrow-leaf evergreens include fir, hemlock, juniper, pine, spruce, yew, cedar, redwood and arborvitae. (Also pruned like narrow-leaf evergreens are dawn redwood, larch, and golden larch even though these narrow-leaf trees are deciduous.) Many people never prune their evergreens, assuming that the plants can take care of themselves. The truth is that they can benefit from occasional pruning to shape and control growth.

New growth on evergreens occurs rapidly over several weeks in the spring. It's important to watch for this growth if you plan to pinch and shape your tree. After the new growth forms, any cuts you make do not heal well. Also, if you wait until buds form at the tip of the new growth and then prune them off, an ugly stub remains until the following spring. Happily, hemlock and juniper have slightly longer growing seasons than other evergreens, giving you more time to prune them before new growth stops. Yews have a second flush of growth in late summer, providing a second opportunity for pruning.

Most evergreens will not grow new branches from old wood or along the trunk. Do not remove entire branches unless you are sure you can live with the look; the branches won't grow back. If you must remove whole limbs, avoid pruning them in the spring when the sap is moving through the tree. Otherwise the tree will bleed profusely. Also, many evergreens have well-developed branch collars. Be sure to cut up to, but not into, the collar.

**Juniper** Junipers grow from buds at the tips of branches and along the stems. You can cut them back just about anywhere there is foliage, but don't prune into bare wood where there are no buds to sprout. Other evergreens to prune this way include arborvitae, oriental arborvitae, cypress, bald cypress, false cypress, redwood, dawn redwood, giant sequoia, incense cedar, and podocarpus.

**Pine** In the spring, pines form upright *candles*—compact new growth that elongates later during the season. Prune candles while they are growing in the spring to force bushier growth. You can also head back long branches to side branches, forcing lateral buds to grow, for a fuller, more compact tree. Never prune a pine back into bare wood. It does not have buds for new growth in this area.

**Spruce** Spruce trees grow much like pines, but you can prune them farther back on the branch. Spruces normally grow symmetrically and need little pruning. Occasionally you need to cut a wayward branch back to a side branch to maintain a symmetrical shape. Again, never cut back into bare wood.

**Yew** Yews sprout from bare wood so you can prune them any way you wish and they will sprout new growth. It is preferable, though, to cut to foliage, and not bare wood, so there are no stubs showing before new growth begins. Prune them formally in hedges or as topiary, or allow them to grow into their natural shape. Treat hemlock similarly.

# SHEARING NARROW-LEAF EVERGREENS

Shearing is a way to shape a plant into smooth planes by cutting across the surface uniformly. It is used to create hedges and green walls or to formalize the shape and density of a pyramidal evergreen tree.

Arborvitae, hemlock, spruce and yew are all excellent choices for shearing. Many evergreens lose their lower limbs over time, but these do not. With careful attention they can make beautiful, solid walls of greenery. Hemlock and yew are especially easy to work with because they sprout from old wood, so you can shear them back just about anywhere. Arborvitae and spruce, along with most other evergreens, will not sprout from old wood; always shear these so that there is still foliage left behind the cut.

Your shearing technique depends on how much you want your hedge or tree to grow, if at all. Shearing each season significantly reduces the ultimate size of the plant. Shear off just the branch tips if you simply want to shape the plant and make it fuller; cut off half the new growth if you want to slow growth a bit; or snip off all new growth if you do not want the plant to grow much larger. For a tight, compact form, shear two or three times during the brief spring growing period.

It is important, when shearing, to keep the top of the plant slightly narrower than the base so the upper limbs do not shade the lower limbs. See pages 26–27.

Heavy shearing often creates a problem called *shear burn,* in which the tender, newly uncovered needles behind the cut turn brown in hot, dry weather. To prevent shear burn, shear more often, but lightly, or prune in damp, overcast weather.

# EVERGREEN SHRUBS

## PRUNING BROADLEAF EVERGREENS

There are many different broadleaf evergreen shrubs. A few of the most common are azalea, boxwood, camellia, holly, mountain laurel, pieris, rhododendron and skimmia. There are also a number of shrubs that are evergreen in warm climates and deciduous in cold climates. These include abelia, some azaleas, cotoneaster, privet and many viburnums. In general, all of these plants do well with very little pruning. If you need to remove dead or broken branches or thin out overgrown plants, the best time to make major cuts is in late winter, before spring growth begins. If you are shaping the plant by pinching or light pruning, do this after the flowers fade on blooming shrubs and in late spring on nonblooming shrubs.

Blooming broadleaf evergreens look best if you remove the spent flowers, a technique known as *deadheading*. It's important to be especially careful when deadheading rhododendron, pieris and mountain laurel because growth buds lie just behind the flowers. Break off the spent flowers gently with your fingers, taking care not to rip off these buds.

Both azalea and boxwood respond well to shearing because they sprout new growth from just about anywhere on the branch. Both plants make good hedges or topiary. Azaleas are especially striking because of their blossoms, but be sure to halt your shearing efforts by mid summer to let flower buds develop. These buds are fatter than foliage buds.

### Formal Hedge Pruning

**First**  To shape a hedge, such as this *Ligustrum* privet, visualize its finished height and prune from the top until you reach it. An electric hedge trimmer is quick and easy—but take care not to cut too much.

**Next**  Step back periodically to check your work. Too much touch-up work results in a hedge that is too short.

**Last**  Shear the sides at an outward slant, making the base wider than the top. This allows plenty of light to reach the lower branches so they stay full and green.

**Natural-Shape Pruning**

**First** Evaluate the plant, in this case a juniper. Overgrown, dense bushes tend to die out in the center and at the base. Wayward branches can ruin the outline of the plant.

**Next** Thin foliage by removing entire branches right to the trunk. Leave bottom branches, or the shrub's base will be bare.

**Last** Step back after thinning and check the outline of the plant. Head back overlong branches that break up a pleasing profile.

# PRUNING NARROW-LEAF EVERGREEN SHRUBS

Shrubs with needles or very narrow, needle-like leaves include arborvitae, hemlock, juniper, spruce and yew. They are generally low-growing species or varieties of narrow-leaf evergreen trees, so pruning them is essentially the same. The biggest difference is that many of the shrubs do not grow very large, so they may never need any pruning at all. This explains why they are so popular—they're easy.

Occasionally, even these easy-care plants benefit from some pruning. In cold-winter areas, this is usually to remove broken or dead branches after a severe winter. In warmer climates, it is more likely that you'll need to prune to thin out or open up an overly dense shrub. As with narrow-leaf evergreen trees, do this type of major pruning any time other than spring.

For a fuller, bushier plant, pinch the tips of the new growth on evergreens. This causes the buds behind the cut to start growing. Do this light pruning in the spring when the plant starts actively growing.

Hemlock and yew make great hedges because they sprout new growth readily no matter how far back you cut. If you cut off a lower branch, new growth fills in the hole. Most other evergreens grow again only from wood with some foliage on it. Do not prune junipers back into old growth even if there is some foliage on the branch; they often do not have any buds this far back to grow new leaves, and you will end up with a stump. If you prune large branches off an overgrown juniper, remember that they will not grow again. Many times gardeners cut off the lower branches of a juniper and find they have created a gaping hole at the plant's base. It's better to cut back a few branches in the middle to thin out the plant, and make it look more open, than to create a bare trunk at the base of a shrub.

# DECIDUOUS SHRUBS

## WHAT ARE THEY?

A deciduous shrub loses its leaves in the fall, is dormant in the winter, and sprouts new green growth in the spring. It is different from an evergreen shrub, which retains its leaves even when dormant. There are also some deciduous shrubs that remain evergreen in mild climates. Some of these are listed on page 26. Most deciduous shrubs are broadleaved. There are very few narrow-leaf deciduous shrubs.

There are many deciduous shrubs. Some are valued for their decorative flowers, while others are especially colorful in fall. A few, including barberry, smoke tree, hawthorn, winterberry, pyracantha (or firethorn) and rugosa rose, are grown for their attractive fruit. (Deciduous shrubs with edible fruit, such as blueberries and raspberries, are covered later in the book.) You can grow many deciduous shrubs as small trees too.

The time of year to prune deciduous shrubs depends partly on the aspect of the plant you most enjoy—flowers, fruit or fall foliage. You want to encourage your favorite part, not inadvertently prune that part away.

Heavily prune deciduous shrubs grown strictly for their foliage in late winter. This includes removing dead or diseased wood or opening up an overgrown plant. Prune lightly and pinch to increase fullness in the spring. Pinch the tips of branches when the shrub is actively growing so you direct the growth to side buds. Because of their interesting branch patterns, some of these shrubs make attractive hedges even while leafless in the wintertime. A few good choices for deciduous hedges include barberry, buckthorn, dwarf ninebark, hedge maple, hornbeam, privet and viburnum.

This lovely deciduous shrub is the lilac *Syringa vulgaris*.

## Pruning a Deciduous Flowering Shrub

**First**  A lilac blooms on old wood in the spring so you prune it in early summer after the flowers fade.

**Next**  Every 3–5 years you need to cut out about 1/3 of the lilac's growth. At the base of the plant, thin out most of the sucker growth and any very old trunks.

**Last**  For good flower production next year, cut off flowers when they fade. Head back any overlong shoots to create a pleasing shape.

# DECIDUOUS FLOWERING SHRUBS

These shrubs exhibit the most dramatic seasonal changes. They are covered with colorful flowers in spring or summer, leafed-out and green through summer and often clothed with fall color in autumn. Although leafless in winter, many of these shrubs have attractive bark or colorful branches. Of these displays, the flowers are usually the showiest.

The first question to ask before you prune a flowering shrub is whether it flowers in spring or summer. If you don't know the answer, find out by watching the plant, checking a plant encyclopedia or asking at your local nursery. Without this information, it is easy to chop off this year's crop of flowers.

Shrubs either bloom in the spring from buds that grew last year and have been dormant all winter, or they bloom in the summer on new growth produced this spring. If they bloom in the early spring, wait until the flowers fade before you prune anything. These blossoms are growing from wood that grew last summer and you don't want to prune all this wood off before the flowers appear. When you prune after the flowers fade, the plant has all summer to produce new growth with buds for next year's flowers.

If your shrubs flower later in the season after leaves appear, the buds are developing on new wood and you need to prune in late winter or very early spring so that lots of new wood grows in the spring. The sequence for pruning flowering shrubs is something that many gardeners have to stop and think about each year before they prune.

Just remember:

- Spring flowering on old wood = summer pruning after flowers fade.
- Summer flowering on new wood = spring pruning before new growth begins.

29

# RENEWING OLD SHRUBS

## WHAT NEEDS RENEWING?

Good candidates for renewal are old shrubs that have grown too tall or wide for their space, those that are so dense the foliage has died on the inside, or those that are too sparse or have too few flowers.

When to renew depends on the type of shrub you have. See the preceding pages for advice. Most overgrown plants need lots of pruning, so spread the job over two or three years. Remember never cut out more than one-third of a plant's foliage at a time or it becomes susceptible to disease and winter injury. Some plants, such as abelia, buddleia and some hydrangeas defy this one-third-a-year rule because you can shear them off almost to the ground in late winter for drastic size reduction. They respond with a burst of new growth in the spring.

If the plant is too tall, you need to reduce its height by cutting the upper branches back or you can remove the upper part of the main stem back to a side branch. The bare space on the top of the plant fills in as you pinch back new growth to force side buds during the growing season. Conversely, you can transform an overgrown shrub with a main trunk into an attractive small tree by removing all the lower branches over time.

Shrubs that are so dense that the foliage is only on the outside benefit from thinning cuts that open up the plant and allow some light inside. This encourages growth in the shrub's interior. Leggy shrubs with sparse foliage respond well when you pinch the branch tips back during the growing season. Lateral buds grow along the sides of the branches and fill in the open spaces.

Shape this *Viburnum burkwoodii* by cutting out old or dead wood.

## Reducing Size

**First** Shrubs, such as this pittosporum, that cover windows or destroy the balance of the landscape because of their height need careful pruning.

**Next** A severe thinning cut that removes all growth above a strong side branch is usually necessary on single-trunked shrubs. Head back multistemmed bushes to the desired height. Some thinning and shaping may be needed.

**Last** The pruned shrub may need some shaping in the following year. If the shrub is extremely overgrown, you will need to make more cuts to reduce height.

## Revitalizing and Opening Up

**First** As seen with this deutzia, foliage cannot grow in the interior of a shrub if it is so dense that light cannot penetrate to the inner branches.

**Next** Thin out branches along the trunk or at the ground level if the new branches all originate at the base.

**Last** Light now penetrates the interior of the plant. Continue the revitalizing process with more thinning cuts next year.

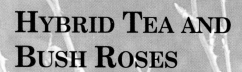

# HYBRID TEA AND BUSH ROSES

In most climates, you can prune your hybrid tea and other modern bush roses anytime from fall through late winter, while they are dormant. However, in very cold climates it is best to wait until early spring, just as new growth begins, so you can see what survived on the plant. In all but the warmest climates the plants are leafless in winter, making this the preferred pruning time because it's easier to see what you are doing.

**Crossing branches**

**Diseased or dead wood**

**Bud union**

## How to Prune

**First** Clear out dead and diseased wood and crossing and weak branches. Cut past the dead wood into healthy, cream-colored wood. For large, showy flowers, a hybrid tea can be cut back safely to just 3 or 4 main canes, but if you want a larger plant, leave more or even all of the healthy canes.

**Last** Head back remaining branches to outward-facing buds. The plant should have a low, open pattern of vigorous branches. When you cut flowers to take indoors, always try to leave 2 leaves with 5 leaflets each on the stem behind the cut. New shoots with more blooms grow from the bases of these leaves.

# PRUNING BASICS

Prune hybrid tea, grandiflora, floribunda, polyantha, miniature and tree roses in the same manner. They bloom on new wood produced each spring, so prune in winter while they are dormant. The main objective when pruning a rose is to remove old growth and keep the plant to the size you choose. By clearing out old branches and shaping roses you encourage new growth and better flowering. Roses do not fit the rule that you should remove only one-third of the plant a year. Often you need to prune much more than this.

Roses vary in their cold hardiness, and in cold climates rose pruning involves cutting out the winter-damaged wood each year. If the winter was severe, there may be little else to prune. In warmer climates if growth is strong, you may have to remove a lot of a vigorous plant each year just to keep the size and shape you desire. Start by removing the oldest *canes* (stems) right to the base of the plant, above the enlarged *bud union* (the place where the bush was grafted to its rootstock). A tree rose has two bud unions— one at the base of the trunk and one at the top. Never prune below the upper bud union (except to remove suckers), or the rose variety grafted to the top will be lost.

On all of these roses, leave most of the newer, greener canes, removing only those that are crowded, damaged or crossing each other. Next, reduce the overall size of the shrub by cutting back all remaining canes to a height that suits your landscape.

When you cut back a cane to shorten it, always cut at a slant just above a bud. Cut to a bud that is facing out from the plant, so that new growth heads outward.

Suckers are the vigorous shoots that grow from below the bud union. Always remove these. Wearing gloves, grasp the sucker firmly and pull or twist it out. This removes buds at the base of the sucker that are usually left behind if you use shears. These buds will sprout later if you do not remove them.

## PRUNING BASICS

The time to prune these roses depends on their blooming season. Some bloom only in the spring, whereas others bloom twice—once in spring on last year's growth, and again in summer on new growth. If you want the maximum amount of flowering on these plants, it's important to prune at the right times.

A newly planted climber must reach the height you want before you begin to prune. This often takes a couple of years. Once the canes are tall enough, tie them so they grow horizontally. The rose blossoms grow from shoots, or laterals, on horizontal canes. The plant must have canes that are long enough to be trained horizontally before these side shoots develop and good flowering begins. So don't prune off those long canes. There are a few climbers, called pillar roses, that bloom well on vertical stems.

Shrub roses and old garden roses all have an attractive, natural habit and do not require too much pruning. As with any plant, prune out dead and damaged wood and do some light trimming to retain a pleasing shape. Wait to prune plants that bloom only in the spring until after they flower. Prune repeat bloomers in late winter or very early spring, and again in the summer. Some shrubby, old-fashioned roses have very rampant growth and do well if you cut back all the canes to one foot each year. This treatment is unnecessary for most roses.

**Repeat-Blooming Climbers**

**First** These roses, shown prior to pruning, bloom in the spring and then again in the summer. Prune them in late winter. Remove oldest canes, keeping 3–4 vigorous canes. Head back remaining canes by a third. Cut laterals (the side shoots on the canes) back to 2 buds.

**Last** After the first flush of bloom, cut off spent flowers as shown here. In the summer, if new growth begins to get overlong, cut back to 2 sets of 5-leaflet leaves.

## Spring-Blooming Climbers and Other Roses

**First** These all bloom once in the spring. Wait to prune them until they have finished flowering. Ramblers and old-fashioned roses are not grafted, so you can cut them back to the bases of the canes.

**Last** On climbers and ramblers, cut back old or weak canes, leaving 4 or 5 vigorous, strong ones. Prune laterals, side shoots, to 4 or 5 sets of leaves. If you desire, severely thin and head back old-fashioned roses.

## Repeat-Blooming Shrub Roses

**First** These roses bloom throughout the spring and summer in flushes. The main pruning is done in late winter, by removing oldest canes and heading back to desired height.

**Last** As the plant continues to bloom, cut off spent flowers. Head back new growth in the summer to no fewer than 2 sets of 5-leaflet leaves.

# ORNAMENTAL VINES

## CLINGING VERSUS TWINING VINES

A vine has one of two ways to climb: it either twines or it clings. The majority of vines twine, or wrap their shoots around the closest support. This should be a trellis, a post or the structure of your choice—but it can just as easily be a ladder, a swing set, or the closest plant if you are not paying attention during the growing season. Some twining vines occasionally need to be tied to their support, and they must be tied to something if you want them to cover a smooth surface such as a wall or fence. Common twining vines include clematis, honeysuckle, ivy, silver lace vine, star jasmine and wisteria.

Clinging vines support themselves by means of tendrils, rootlets or sucker discs. Tendrils wrap tightly around any support they touch: trellises, wires or plants. Grapes climb using tendrils. Rootlets and sucker discs, on the other hand, need no added support because they adhere tightly to walls and fences. The rootlets are sometimes known as *holdfasts*—an apt name because they can be difficult to remove. Sucker discs are just as strong.

The most common clinging vines with rootlets or sucker discs are climbing hydrangea, Boston ivy and English ivy. These plants are not a good choice for wood fences or homes with wood siding or shingles. They attach so tightly that removing them leaves the rootlets or discs behind and if you want to paint the wood, you must cut the vines down; you cannot reattach them.

A few plants that are considered vines, such as climbing roses and bougainvillea, do not twine or cling and therefore need to be tied to their supports as new branches grow.

**Pruning Vines**

**First** Prune a summer-flowering vine in the late winter or early spring while the plant is still dormant or the buds are just beginning to swell. A heavily overgrown plant needs untangling and thinning. The side shoots need heading back to control growth and encourage flowering.

**Then** One of the toughest jobs is untangling an overgrown vine. It takes some patience to cut carefully and remove the pruned material. Follow the branch back to its point of origin, cut, then chop the pruned branch into several pieces to untangle and remove it easily. If you cut and remove without checking, you may create some gaping holes that take all season to fill in again.

**Third** Prune side shoots back to 2 buds. This keeps the vine from becoming an overgrown mass again. If healthy, both buds will produce plenty of foliage with flowers.

**Last** A well-pruned vine looks a bit bare when you finish, but once the plant begins to grow you can enjoy the fruits of your labor. An open, leafy plant with loads of flowers is far more appealing than an overgrown mass of greenery with few blooms.

# TIME TO PRUNE

Gardeners grow most vines for their ornamental flowers. A few exceptions are English ivy and Boston ivy. English ivy is an evergreen and you can prune it anytime during the growing season from spring to fall. Boston ivy is deciduous so you can do the major pruning in late winter or early spring and then shape and control growth during the growing season as needed.

Ivy vines grow very fast and become thick walls of greenery over just a few years. Prune them heavily, thinning to keep an open, more attractive look. If they get completely out of hand, cut them to the ground and allow them to start over. Select just a few new vines from the regrowth and cut out all others. Prune heavily to avoid repeating the process in a few years.

Flowering vines, just like flowering shrubs, bloom either in the spring on last year's wood or in the summer on new growth produced that spring. This, of course, dictates when it is best to prune your vines. Prune spring flowering vines after the plant is through blooming. In the summer new wood grows and forms flower buds that overwinter. Then they bloom the following spring. Allow them to grow new wood that will bloom next year. Prune your summer-flowering vines in late winter or early spring. They bloom on new growth from this spring. They respond to pruning with lots of new growth and this growth then produces the flowers. You can lightly trim and shape summer-flowering vines in the summer or early fall after the blooms fade without hindering next year's flower crop. Just remember that in colder climates new growth stimulated by a late pruning can be damaged by an early frost. If you live in a cold climate, wait until early spring to prune.

# FAVORITE VINES

## WISTERIA

Wisteria produces pendulous clusters of purple, pink or white flowers in spring just as the vine begins to leaf out.

The vine blooms on last year's wood. The blossoms emerge from fat buds growing on short spurs. New buds develop in the summer, remain through winter and bloom the following spring.

Normally you would prune a plant of this type in the summer after the flowers fade, but because it is such a fast grower, you can prune wisteria in the winter and again in the summer. In the late winter, prune back long, unwanted side branches, tangled growth and old flower stems and pods. Do not cut off spurs with flower buds. You can trim the branchlets on these spurs to four or five buds as shown, to stimulate larger flowers.

In the summer, allow new shoots to grow in the direction you desire and cut off all others. Leave flowering spurs with their fat buds alone. You can prune wisteria severely without harming the plant.

Occasionally a mature wisteria vine fails to bloom. If this happens, do not fertilize the plant in the spring. You can cut into the root zone with a shovel, in late spring, to prune the roots and cause some stress to the plant. This sometimes stimulates blooming.

Prune this *Wisteria floribunda* in winter and summer to control growth.

## Pruning Clematis

**Spring-flowering** After blooms fade, cut back heavily to encourage new growth and bud formation for the following spring.

**Summer-flowering** In late winter, trim stems back or right to the ground. In cold climates, wait until buds show green.

**Twice-flowering** After spring bloom, cut back to encourage second bloom. In late winter, lightly prune and shape.

# CLEMATIS

Clematis is a deciduous vine that bursts forth in the spring or summer with showy blossoms, often up to six inches across. The flowers bloom in white, yellow, pink, red, magenta, purple or blue. Without the flowers, the vine is unexceptional, but the spectacular blooming period makes the plant more than worthwhile.

There are three types of flowering clematis: those that bloom once in the spring on last year's growth, those that bloom once in the summer on new wood and those that bloom twice—once in the spring on last year's growth and again in the summer on new growth. The type you grow dictates the best pruning method. Before you despair of ever sorting this out, be assured that clematis plants are rampant growers. If you prune one incorrectly, it will probably still flower well. Established plants cut to the ground grow and flower the following spring or summer. Correct pruning just gives you a chance to get the most in form and flower from your vine.

Spring-flowering clematis vines bloom on wood that grew the summer before. Prune them after the flowers are through—this encourages new growth that will bloom even more the following year.

Summer-flowering plants bloom on new stems that grew during the current spring. Prune these in the late winter, or when the buds swell, but before new growth starts.

Twice-blooming clematis plants flower on old wood in the spring and again on new shoots in the late summer. In the winter dormant season, prune to untangle and thin the plant—but keep your pruning light or you will cut off most of the buds for spring flowers. After spring flowering is past, prune heavily to encourage lots of new growth that can bloom later in the season.

# FRUITS AND NUTS

## THE YOUNG PLANT

Trees, shrubs and vines grown for their edible fruit need careful pruning for optimum growth and production. If you start when the plant is young, you keep the job of pruning simple and the plant produces a yearly crop of delicious fruit.

Of all fruiting plants, trees are the most important to prune correctly from the beginning because branch structure is very difficult to change as the tree grows older. There are two pruning phases: training for the first few years, and then yearly pruning throughout the plant's life. The next few pages describe specific pruning methods for the most popular fruiting plants.

Most fruit trees are sold in *bare-root* form—with no soil around the roots. A bare-root tree, called a *whip,* looks like a stick with a few roots attached. It may or may not have some branches. Trees in containers or with burlap around the rootball are more likely to have received their early pruning at the nursery.

If there are no branches on the whip, trim any broken roots, plant it in the ground, and head back the top to two to three feet. If there are branches on your newly planted tree, prune them to one or two buds. Cut to outward facing buds. New growth develops along the trunk through the summer.

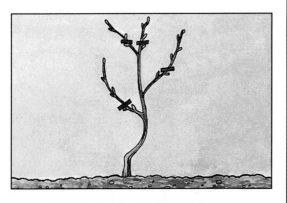

## Early Open-Center Pruning

**First Winter**  Choose 3 or 4 branches spaced about 6 in. apart and not directly above one another. Head these branches back to 2–3 ft., leaving the highest branch the longest. Cut off all other wood, including the leader.

**Second Summer**  Head back overlong or drooping branches early in the season. Remove any damaged wood, water sprouts or root suckers that develop (see pgs. 10–11).

**Second Winter**  Prune to 1 or 2 secondary branches on the main laterals. Try to select branches that fill out the overall shape of the tree.

**Mature Fruit Tree Shapes**

**Open Center** The goal for this shape is to keep the tree low to the ground and allow sunlight to reach the foliage.

**Modified Central Leader** Similar to open center, only scaffold branches emerge at 4–7 ft. on the trunk. If the tree is not tall enough the first winter, wait until the second winter to select scaffolds.

**Central Leader** Choose the lowest limb desired and remove limbs below. Select about 4 well-spaced limbs up the trunk and cut out others. Keep the central leader the longest.

# MATURE FRUIT TREE SHAPES

When pruned correctly from the start, a mature fruit tree usually has one of three shapes: *open center, modified central leader,* or *central leader.*

Pruning for an open center, sometimes called the *vase method,* is a technique used commonly on apricots, cherries, figs, nectarines, peaches, pears and plums, and occasionally on apples. Three or four main branches all emerge very close together from the lower three feet of the trunk. As the tree grows, you prune branches to outside buds to keep the center of the tree open. There is little central trunk, just large branches forming a vase shape from the base of the tree. This shape allows sunlight to reach the interior of the tree, which increases fruit production.

The modified central leader method is often used for tall trees like walnut and pecan, and is also a good choice for apples and pears. The pruning is the same as for an open-center tree but the main trunk grows up about four or five feet before you select lateral branches. The branches are higher off the ground, leaving more room to walk under, and the center of the tree gets plenty of sunlight.

With the central leader method you allow the tree to grow with a strong central trunk and space the scaffold branches evenly up and down and around it. Many standard-sized apples and pears are trained this way because they bear heavy crops that can break weak branches. The branch structure is strong on a central leader tree. The only problem with this shape is that if the tree grows too tall, the fruit is out of reach and the top of the central leader occasionally bends under its weight. If this occurs, you may need to cut back the leader to a side branch. The best way to avoid this is to select dwarf fruit trees at planting time.

Once you create the tree's basic structure, prune it according to its type, as described in the next pages.

# APPLE TREES

Apples grow on spurs that bear fruit for many years. Pick the fruit carefully so you don't accidentally pull off the spur. If the spur is removed, no more apples will grow at that spot.

Make heading cuts (red) and thinning cuts (black) to maintain the size and shape you desire for the tree.

Fire blight is a bacterial disease that spreads rapidly on infected plants and kills them. Apples and pears are very susceptible. Wood looks black and burnt; leaves turn brown, then black. Immediately prune a foot below the area with tools you have disinfected with a bleach solution (one part bleach diluted with ten parts water) before each cut. Dispose of diseased material to prevent further spread.

## Pruning Basics

Apples are among the longest-lived fruit trees, surviving in some gardens for generations. They are easy to prune and can be shaped using any of the three basic methods: open, modified central leader or central leader.

The apples grow on spurs that develop on two-year-old wood. The spurs bear fruit for many years, and only a very drastic pruning can eliminate all of them from a mature tree. The flowers and fruit develop at the end of the spur, which then grows a bit off to the side of the fruit and produces a bud for next year.

Late winter is the time to prune, before spring growth begins. Cut out all damaged or diseased wood as well as suckers and water sprouts. Prune new growth to keep the branches from shading the center of the tree. Remove crossed or downward-growing branches and head back top branches to reduce height, if needed. When the tree bears only every other year, cut back older, longer spurs to revitalize them. Thin your apple crop in late June; there is often a natural apple drop before this. Heavy thinning results in larger fruit. Leave one apple per spur and space fruits at least six inches apart. Be careful not to pull the spurs off when you thin.

Because a mature apple tree can reach 30 feet, many home gardeners plant dwarf apple trees to conserve space. These trees are grafted to a dwarfing rootstock and there are many varieties available. If the variety grows to only about four feet, use a pruning method known as *spindle bush*. This is basically the central leader method, but since the tree stays so short you begin by cutting the bare-root whip back to just 22 inches tall. Cut side branches to two buds or about three to four inches long. Side branches, or laterals, should move up the trunk like a spiral staircase to allow the greatest exposure to the sun. After you have pruned the side branches, maintain the central leader by cutting back any laterals that grow past it.

# APRICOT TREES

Apricots produce fruit on two-year-old spurs that last for two more years; then you prune them out. This means that the tree needs heavy pruning each year to ensure a good crop. The trick is to know which wood is old and which is new.

**Bud scar**

**Fruiting bud**

**Older branch with spurs**

**This year's new spurs**

Make heading cuts (red) and thinning cuts (black) to maintain the correct size and shape for the tree.

# PRUNING BASICS

Apricot trees live 20 to 30 years, which is a fairly long time for a fruit tree. Properly pruned, an apricot tree provides a wonderful crop of tree-ripe fruit that you simply cannot find at the grocery store. The trees do bloom early; in cold-winter areas the crop can be drastically reduced by late freezes. Most often, young trees are pruned in the open center method. This keeps the fruit low and easy to pick.

The trees bear fruit on two-year-old spurs that then bear for two more years. A spur grows the first year, begins to produce fruit the second year and continues to produce fruit the third and fourth year. After that, fruit production stops. You should cut off the spur to stimulate the growth of new fruiting spurs. Each winter, prune out old wood containing four-year-old finished spurs. The branch section containing these spurs should be the fourth section back from the tip. (Each section begins at a bud scar.) Head back new branches to encourage spur production and to keep the tree vigorous. Heavy pruning brings on lots of new growth which produces new spurs to replace the spent ones.

Because its new growth is headed back yearly, a well-pruned apricot tree looks squat and stumpy rather than graceful and airy. What it lacks in appearance, it more than makes up for in production.

Prune apricot trees in late winter. A good rule is to prune out one-third of the old growth every year as well as one-third off the new shoots. As always, start your pruning by removing any dead or diseased material and any shoots along the base of the trunk. Make sure your pruning allows lots of light into the center of the tree.

Natural thinning occurs when small fruits drop early in their development or if there is a late frost. If the tree sets fruit heavily, thin it to two inches between each fruit.

# BUSH BERRIES

Blueberries, currants and gooseberries are bush berries; they bear fruit on a long-lived shrub. Blackberries and raspberries (discussed on pages 48–49) are cane berries: their fruit grows on long branches or canes that you remove each year so new canes will replace them.

## Pruning Blueberries, Currants and Gooseberries

**First** Cut 3-year-old branches right to the ground. Cut out tangled growth and any dead or diseased material.

**Last** On blueberries, thin branch tips to encourage fewer but larger berries. You can cut off up to 2/3 of a blueberry branch and still get a good crop.

## PRUNING BASICS

All the bush berries make attractive landscape shrubs and need very little pruning. If the plant is vigorous, you can thin the fruit so that the remaining fruits will grow larger. Prune blueberries, currants and gooseberries in late winter or very early spring in the coldest regions.

Blueberries grow slowly at the start and fruit very little for the first few years, but they tend to bear heavily once established. Usually you start pruning about the third year; in harsh climates, it may be later. For the first few years, just remove any dead branches. You can also remove flower buds to encourage the plant to put all energies into growing. After that, do more or less pruning, according to the amount of new growth each year. The fruit grows on one-year-old wood that grows from either two-year-old wood or the base of the plant. If the plant is growing well, prune out three-year-old and older branches right to the ground each year to promote lots of new growth. To encourage larger fruit, head back branch tips with many buds. Thinning fruit is not necessary if you head back these branches.

Currants and gooseberries do best in places where the weather never gets too hot; for this reason they are grown mostly in the North. It is best to plant them in the fall because they leaf out early. Both fruits produce on year-old wood and on spurs of older wood. Although they produce even when ignored and not pruned, the plants look better and the crop is improved if you cut older stems to the ground beginning when the bushes are about three years old. Thinning will not improve the size of currants but it does help on gooseberries. When the fruits are very small, thin gooseberries to one inch apart. (Wear gloves.) Heavy pruning also encourages large fruit in gooseberries.

# CANE BERRIES

All cane berries have perennial roots but the canes last just two years, so pruning them is simply a renewal process. The canes grow in the first year and bear fruit in the second year. After they fruit the second year, cut them out—they do not bear again.

Remove spent 2-year-old canes—such as these boysenberries—in late winter when they are withered and easy to distinguish from new 1-year-old canes that will fruit in the coming summer.

# BLACKBERRIES

There are two types of blackberries. The erect blackberry, sometimes called the rigid type, is the most typical and can stand without support. The other type is the trailing blackberry, which is called the dewberry in the South. On the Pacific coast, popular varieties of trailing blackberry have familiar names like boysenberry and loganberry. These trailing kinds must be tied to some type of support.

In late spring or summer, when new canes on erect blackberries are about two and one-half feet tall, pinch or trim the tips to encourage branching. The following late winter or early spring, cut back the side branches to about 15 inches. Then allow the plant to grow and bear fruit in the summer. The following winter, cut old, withered canes that bore fruit right to the ground. Again, head back tips of new canes when they reach two and one-half feet tall, and begin the cycle again.

Tie trailing blackberries to a trellis or wire as they grow out. Canes fruit during their second summer. The following winter, cut to the ground all canes that bore fruit. As new canes grow, tie them to supports.

When pruning blackberries, always remove dead or diseased material first. If too many new canes grow, thin them back to a manageable number.

Individual fruits do not need to be thinned on cane berry plants.

# RASPBERRIES

Raspberries come in several colors, including red, yellow, purple and black, and they fall into three different groups according to how they grow and bear fruit. The first group is made up of red and yellow raspberries that bear in summer. The second consists of red and yellow raspberries that bear in both fall and summer; these are called everbearing raspberries. All red and yellow types have long, straight canes that stand erect, although they can be tied to supports. Finally, there are the purple and black raspberries, which fruit in summer and branch like erect blackberries. They look like blackberries, too. The way to tell a black raspberry from a blackberry is by pulling it off the stem. A raspberry pulls off completely, leaving a hollow berry. A blackberry retains its core.

Prune summer-bearing red and yellow raspberries in the late winter before new growth starts. Remove withered, two-year-old canes that bore the previous summer and cut back canes from last summer to about four feet. These bear fruit in the coming summer and you cut them out the following winter. Thin the new canes to the number you desire, usually leaving eight inches between them.

Prune everbearing red and yellow raspberries in fall and winter, because they fruit twice. In fall, berries grow on the tops of new canes. After fruiting, prune off the bearing portion of these canes. The following summer, berries will grow on the lower portion. Cut the withered two-year-old canes to the ground in winter.

Prune purple and black raspberries much like erect blackberries. When plants reach two and one-half feet tall in summer, pinch the tips to encourage side branching. In spring, cut back side branches to just one foot. After these branches fruit in summer, cut them off at the ground. Repeat the cycle as this year's canes reach two and one-half feet.

# CHERRY TREES

Cherry trees are either sweet or sour—or a hybrid of the two called Duke. Sweet cherries are very upright in habit and grow quite tall. Sour cherries are shorter and spread wider. Somewhat sweeter Duke cherries grow much like sour cherries, and you prune them the same way.

# Pruning Basics

Cherry trees are available in bush, dwarf or standard-size forms. Most sold at nurseries are grafted to rootstock that keeps them small, since standard trees grow tall enough that the fruit can be too high to reach. Bush cherries, the least common form, are shrubs that can be pruned into hedges. All cherries are lovely when they bloom in the spring.

Cherry trees are easy to prune. All types bear on long-lived spurs so pruning is necessary more to shape the tree than to encourage fruit. Very little pruning is required after the first few years. Fruiting begins the third or fourth year, typically, and it is not necessary to thin the fruit.

Sweet cherries grow mainly vertically, so the early pruning you do is to encourage a more spreading shape. Prune sweet cherries by the open center method. After the first year, in late winter, prune to three or four branches spaced evenly around the tree. These should be about six to eight inches apart vertically. Head back these selected scaffold branches to two to three feet. The following late winter, cut off all but two side branches per scaffold and head these secondary branches to two to three feet. Always cut to outward-facing buds. This establishes the main framework of the tree. Keep the center open to admit plenty of light to the interior.

Sour and Duke cherries need even less pruning than sweet cherries because the trees tend to spread more. It is best to prune using the central leader system. Cut back long branches that outgrow the shape of the tree, and any downward-growing branches.

Every year in late winter, prune out dead or damaged wood and prune a bit to open up the tree and allow sunlight to reach the interior. You may need to thin some of the branches, but keep in mind that too much pruning can weaken the tree.

Make heading cuts (red) and thinning cuts (black) to maintain the size and shape that is correct for the tree.

# CITRUS TREES

A mature citrus tree makes an attractive landscape plant, and the scent of the flowers is strong and delightful. Gardeners in cold climates can grow dwarf types in containers and keep them inside in a sunny south-facing window during the colder months.

The lemon tree is one of the hardiest citrus trees.

# PRUNING BASICS

Where citrus trees thrive, they are easy to care for and their fruit is delicious. Unfortunately, citrus plants cannot survive cold weather. Even light freezes kill all but the toughest lemon trees, and without plenty of heat the fruit does not develop its full sweetness. If you do live in a warm climate, a citrus tree is a great addition to the garden.

The flowers usually bloom in the spring, and fruits set on shoots at the end of the current year's growth. The plant continues to grow past the shoots as the fruit develops. In warm climates, the fruit often matures by fall or winter. The two exceptions are Valencia oranges, which ripen in late spring into summer, and grapefruits, which take 18 months to ripen fully. In cooler climates, all citrus fruits take longer to become sweet. Taste-test one or two before harvesting the whole crop.

Citrus trees of all types require almost no pruning. The bit of pruning you need to do involves cutting out dead material and occasionally thinning fruit if a branch looks as if it might break under the load of the crop. This is not to say that you should not prune citrus trees. They respond well to pruning and can be *espaliered* (trained flat against a wall), or even made into hedges.

If you live in a cold climate, you can grow a citrus plant in a container and move it indoors to a sunny window in the fall. You will probably need to prune it to keep the plant small. Cut overlong branches to side branches to reduce size. Some shaping may also be necessary. Cut back long stems to a leaf to encourage branching and fullness.

Large, vigorous landscape plants respond well to heavy pruning. You may want to reduce the overall size of the tree by heading back branches or removing lower branches to allow movement underneath, whether for walking or mowing. Very heavy pruning reduces the amount of fruit the tree produces for at least a year.

# TRAINING GRAPES

## EARLY PRUNING

The first two years, grapevines need a lot of pruning and training to establish a strong plant. After that, more pruning and training is needed to encourage a good crop of fruit. There are two common methods of pruning mature grapevines: the *spur* method and the *cane* method. Until the second summer, all grapes are pruned alike.

Grapes are fast growers and fruit mostly on shoots that grow on year-old wood. Once the vine is established, canes grow the first year and fruit develops on shoots from that wood the next year. You then prune off these shoots to allow new wood to develop. Each summer there are two stages of growth: last year's canes with fruit, and this year's shoots, which will be next year's canes.

Prune your grapevine for the first time when you plant it. Cut the vine back to five inches tall and cut off all side canes. Allow the plant to grow unchecked through the spring and summer. Late the following winter, prune off all last year's growth along the sides to create a single stem. Secure the stem to a post for several years until the trunk is strong. Set posts eight to ten feet on either side of this main trunk of the vine. Train the lateral canes on wires secured between these posts.

During the second spring, prune back to one main shoot and two side shoots at the level of the first wire. At this point you must choose the type of training that suits the kind of grapevine you are growing (see page 56). Spur pruning develops permanent arms, or *cordons,* on a trunk. Cane pruning develops new arms each season. The pruning and training during the second summer are a bit different for each, as shown at the right.

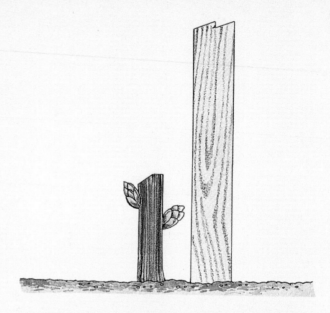

**First Spring** Cut back the newly planted vine to 5 in. leaving at least 2 buds or 2 side canes trimmed to the trunk.

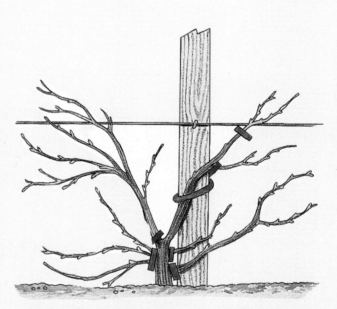

**First Winter** Prune off all side canes and head the main stem at the wire.

54

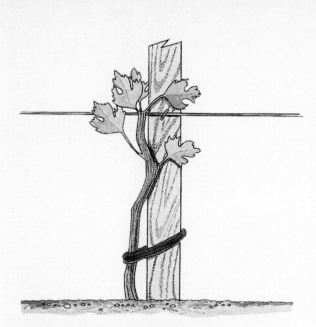

**Second Spring** Cut off all new spring growth to 2 side shoots and one vertical stem.

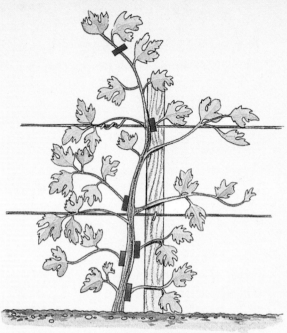

**Second Summer (Cane Pruning)** Cut off the main stem 10 in. above the top wire. Remove all side shoots except those you select to train on the wires; one pair per wire. Thin any fruit that develops.

**Second Summer (Spur Pruning)** Cut off the upright shoot when it reaches the top wire. Train two cordons along each wire and cut off all other growth along the trunk.

# MATURE GRAPES

## SPUR VERSUS CANE

Grapes that grow unpruned develop a lot of foliage but little fruit. If you want a good crop you must prune mature grapevines heavily every winter. You can use one of the two methods shown here.

Most European table-grape and wine-grape varieties respond best when trained using the spur technique. With this method, the long cordons become permanent parts of the vine along with the trunk. Short, knobby canes called spurs develop on the cordons and carry the fruit. Once the vine is established, you cut the spurs to two buds in the winter. Both these buds grow out into canes that bear fruit in the summer. In late winter, cut off the outer cane completely and cut the other to two buds. Again, the two buds grow out and bear fruit in summer. In late winter, you again cut off the outer cane and cut the other cane back to two buds.

American grape varieties, including 'Thompson Seedless', grow best if you use the cane-pruning technique. With this method new canes or cordons grow from the trunk each season and bear fruit the next. Then you cut them off. Once the plant is established, there is always one fruiting cordon and two new cordons, or *renewal canes,* growing out each season. In late winter, cut off the lower cordon that fruited. Prune the outer renewal cane to 12 buds, and the inner renewal cane to just two buds. The following summer, allow the longer renewal cane to bear fruit while the shorter one forms two more renewal canes, one from each bud. That winter, start the cycle again: Cut off the fruiting cane, and prune the two new renewal canes long and short to bear fruit and more renewal canes respectively.

## Spur Pruning

**Second Winter** Cut off main stem where topmost cordons emerge. Cut back all side shoots on cordons and any shoots along the trunk.

**Third Winter** Thin side shoots to 8 in. apart and cut remaining shoots back to 2 buds.

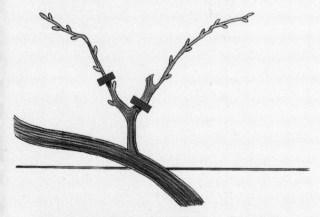

**Fourth and Following Winters** Cut off the outer cane on each spur and cut the other back to 2 buds.

## Cane Pruning

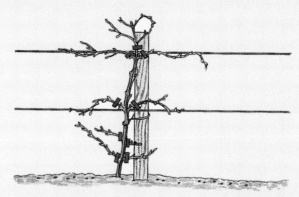

**Second Winter** Cut off main stem just above top wire. Cut shoots back to 2 buds each and remove all other shoots along trunk.

**Third Winter** Two canes grew at each bud forming 2 pairs of canes at each wire. Head back outer cane to 12 buds. This will be the fruiting cane. Head back the other cane to 2 buds to form renewal canes.

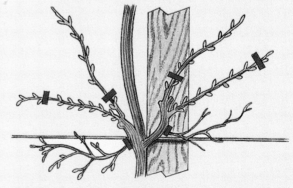

**Fourth and Following Winters** Cut off cane that fruited. Head the outer cane to 12 buds and tie to the wire. Head the other cane to 2 buds.

# PEACH AND NECTARINE TREES

Peaches and nectarines grow only on year-old spurs. Unless the tree is pruned yearly, the fruits grow farther out on the branches every year. This makes them harder to reach and more likely to break off tree limbs with their weight.

These year-old flowering spurs bear fruit this season only. Next year the trees will bear fruit on spurs that grew farther out on the branch this year.

## Pruning Basics

Peaches and nectarines require more pruning than any of the other fruit trees. They grow fast and they fruit on year-old wood. This means you must cut them back severely, late each winter, if you want to keep the tree size manageable and the fruit within reach. Open-center pruning is the best way to accomplish this.

After planting in the spring, prune a bare-root peach or nectarine whip back to two feet tall, first making sure that there are buds below this point. The following winter, select three branches radiating symmetrically from the trunk and cut each back to an outward-facing bud. Prune off all other branches at the trunk. The following (or second) winter, cut out any diseased or dead wood and any crossing branches or upright stems. Shorten the remaining branches by one-third. Each subsequent winter, repeat this procedure. If there are few diseased, crossed or upright branches, remove two out of three branches and then head back the remainder by one-third. You must remove a total of two-thirds of the tree each year to prune properly.

Commonly, these trees set too much fruit and you need to thin to get a good crop of large peaches or nectarines. When the fruit is about the size of your thumbnail, thin to six to eight inches between fruits.

Dwarf peach and nectarine trees are very popular for small gardens. These shrubby plants reach only five to seven feet and need little pruning. In late winter, do a clean-up pruning of dead or diseased wood and upright branches. You may need to prune out some branches to keep the center of the tree open to the light.

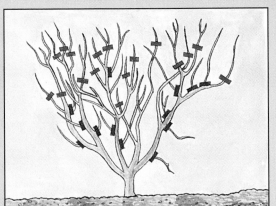

Make heading cuts (red) and thinning cuts (black) to maintain the size and shape that is correct for the tree.

# Pear Trees

Pears are one of the few fruits that do not ripen on the tree. You pick the fruit when it is still green and allow it to ripen in a warm, dry spot. Keep pears out of direct sun while they develop their soft, juicy flesh.

Use wedges or spreader boards during the growing season to increase and strengthen branch angles. Without some help, pears naturally form narrow, weak crotches that break easily in wind and under the weight of a crop.

Spurs on pear trees bear fruit for many years.

## PRUNING BASICS

Pears are quite easy to prune. Like apples, they bear fruit on spurs that last for many years and only severe pruning can remove a crop.

The trees grow very upright, so prune to encourage a more spreading tree with stronger branch angles. The open center method of pruning works best for pear trees, although you can also use the modified central leader method.

At planting time in the spring, cut the bare-root whip back to two and one-half feet. Shorten any branches below this cut to two- to four-inch stubs. Because the branches tend to grow vertically, make all pruning cuts to outward-facing buds to help develop a wider tree. Select scaffold branches with the widest angle of attachment. (See pages 10–11.) After you have established the framework, much of your pruning will be in the upper portion of the tree. That winter, cut upper branches back to laterals. Prune lower branches lightly; too much pruning weakens them. At this time it is also a good idea to cut back some of the new growth at the top of the tree to reduce its height.

Many dwarf varieties of pear are available. Because these are small trees, prune them using the central leader method. They also make attractive espalier plants when trained against a trellis or fence. Pears, like apples, are very susceptible to the disease called fire blight. If you see any stems or leaves that are blackened as if they were burned, prune them out immediately. Cut a foot below the infection into healthy wood. (See page 42.)

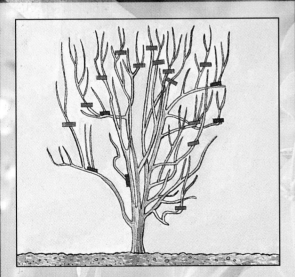

Make heading cuts (red) and thinning cuts (black) to maintain the size and shape that is correct for the tree.

# PLUM TREES

There are two types of plums—Japanese and European—and you prune them differently. Prunes are a type of European plum that you should treat in the same manner. If you have a small space, choose dwarf or bush variety plum trees.

# PRUNING BASICS

Both types of plums bear fruit on long-lived lateral spurs. Because the spurs bear for many years, the trees are relatively easy to prune as long as you do not remove all the spurs with a drastic pruning job. It is also important to pick the ripe fruit carefully so you don't damage or tear off the spurs. The trees do best if you prune by the open center method, with three or four wide-angled limbs around the trunk. As with most fruiting plants, prune in late winter or early spring before new growth begins.

European plums, including prunes, need the least pruning. Remove upright stems; also cut off branches with narrow angles of attachment.

Japanese plums grow on very vigorous trees that need much pruning to keep them in good shape. In the late winter you must thin the growth. Begin by removing vertical branches. Then cut back overlong shoots. Periodically you can head back the top of the tree to shorten it and keep the fruit within reach.

Occasionally, prune trees and both types of plum trees need new spurs. Allow some shoots to go without being pruned every few years. After two to three years this growth carries new spurs. You can head these branches back a bit at this time to shape the tree. Just don't cut them off completely or all your new spurs will be gone, too.

When the fruits are still tiny, thin them to five inches apart for a good crop of large fruit.

Black knot is a disease that infects some types of plums, especially the European varieties. Saplike material oozes along small branches, which you must prune out immediately. After each cut, disinfect your pruning shears with bleach diluted with ten parts water. Throw away the pruned parts to prevent any further spread.

Make heading cuts (red) and thinning cuts (black) to maintain the size and shape that is correct for the tree.

# PECAN AND WALNUT TREES

Pecans are pruned to a central leader, and once the branch pattern is established they require little pruning beyond shaping and removing deadwood. The same is true if you are growing a walnut tree just for beauty. However, for a good crop of walnuts, you must do some early training and a bit more maintenance pruning each year.

The black walnut tree is usually grown for its landscape beauty rather than its nut bounty.

## PRUNING BASICS

Two types of walnut tree are commonly grown—the black walnut, which has extremely hard husks around the nut and often is grown as a landscape tree, and the English walnut, which is also attractive but is grown more commonly for its fruit. English walnut trees are often grafted onto rootstock of the more disease-resistant black walnut.

If you are growing a walnut tree just for beauty, prune it using the central leader method and maintain this shape over the years. Pecans, too, need only this minimal treatment.

Walnuts are large trees, and the nuts grow on long-lived spurs. Harvesting the crop is easy, even on a tall, mature tree, because the nuts fall to the ground when ripe.

Walnuts and pecans differ from many fruiting plants in that you prune them in summer or in autumn after the nuts have fallen. Most of the pruning is done to establish an open, healthy framework; after that little pruning is needed.

Train walnut trees by the central leader method in the first few years. This is the strongest shape and walnuts often bear such heavy crops that the young tree needs to be strong. After a few years you can prune to create the modified central leader shape.

By the first autumn the tree should be over six feet tall. Cut it off to a bud at six feet. If it has not grown enough, wait another year. The following year after heading to six feet, cut back any branches below five feet and begin to select main scaffolds above this point. The reason you cut the lower branches back to short stubs, and not off, is to allow some leaves to develop along the trunk. Walnut trunks burn easily in hot sun and these leaves shade and protect them.

Over the next few years, select four to six scaffold branches in a spiral up the trunk. As the tree matures, prune it to remove dead or diseased wood, suckers and heavy growth in the center of the tree.

Make heading cuts (red) and thinning cuts (black) to maintain the size and shape that is correct for the tree.

# PRUNING CHART

Use this chart to gather details about a particular plant. Follow the guidelines on how to prune, referring back to the technique descriptions in the book. If you only know the common name, check the index for cross-reference.

| PRUNING CHART CODES | PLANT TYPE |
|---|---|
| Broadleaf tree | BT |
| Flowering tree | FLT |
| Fruiting tree | FT |
| Grass | G |
| Narrow-leaf tree | NT |
| Evergreen shrub | ES |
| Partially evergreen shrub | PES |
| Deciduous shrub | DS |
| Vine | V |

| *Botanical name,* common name | Plant Type | Pruning Goal | When to Prune | How to Prune |
|---|---|---|---|---|
| *Abelia* species, abelia | ES, PES, DS | open, arching shape | late winter | Thin out old growth. Cold regions: cut to 4". |
| *Abies* species, fir | NT | remove deadwood | summer | Cut to trunk or closest branch behind deadwood. |
| *Abutilon* species, flowering maple | ES | fullness, shaping | late winter | Thin old growth. Pinch tips. |
| *Acacia* species, acacia, wattle | FLT, ES, DS | thin and shape | anytime | Remove old, dead or crowded branches. |
| *Acer* species, maple | BT, ES, DS | good branch structure | anytime but spring | Remove badly placed branches. |
| *Actinidia* species, kiwi | V | thin, untangle | late winter | Cut back to 2 or 3 new buds. |
| *Aesculus* species, horsechestnut, buckeye | BT DS | train to single trunk rejuvenate | late winter late winter | Remove growth at base, shape. Trim out oldest growth. |
| *Ailanthus altissima,* tree-of-heaven | BT | thin and shape | winter | Pull off suckers, prune damaged branches. |
| *Albizia julibrissin,* silk tree, mimosa | BT | train and shape | early spring, summer | Can train for single or multiple trunks. |
| *Allamanda cathartica,* common allamanda | V | thin and untangle | late winter, late spring | Pinch and head back to form vine or shrub. |
| *Alnus* species, alder | BT | good branch structure | late winter | Remove suckers and deadwood. |
| *Amelanchier* species, shadbush | BT, DS | clean up, shape | late winter | Cut out deadwood, crossing branches. |
| *Amorpha fruticosa,* false indigo | DS | shape, open up | late winter | Prune out oldest stems yearly. |
| *Ampelopsis* species, blueberry climber | V | shape, thin out | early spring, summer | Cut out unwanted growth and shorten stems. |
| *Anemopaegma chamberlaynii,* yellow trumpet vine | V | control shape and size | after summer flowers | Thin and detangle. Shorten long stems. |
| *Angophora costata,* gum myrtle | BT | train to good shape | late winter | Select strong scaffold branches; prune out excess. |
| *Anisacanthus thurberi,* desert honeysuckle | ES, DS | encourage new growth | winter | Cut to ground or shorten branches drastically. |
| *Annona cherimola,* cherimoya | DS | shape and open up | when leafless | Remove lower branches and thin interior. |
| Apple | FT | shape and keep open | late winter | See pages 42–43. |
| Apricot | FT | renew fruit spurs | late winter | See pages 44–45. |
| *Aralia* species, aralia | BT, DS | keep open | late winter–summer | Thin out at base, cut out deadwood. |
| *Araucaria* species, monkey-puzzle, Norfolk Island pine | NT | little pruning needed | anytime | Head wayward growth to branch pair or trunk. |
| *Arbutus unedo,* strawberry tree | BT | little pruning needed | early spring | Trim to shape. |
| *Arctostaphylos* species, manzanita | ES | little pruning needed | spring | Pinch tips to shape, cut out deadwood. |
| *Aristolochia durior,* Dutchman's-pipe | V | control growth | after flowering | Detangle and thin. Can be cut to ground. |
| *Aronia* species, chokeberry | DS | thin, control growth | late winter | Cut old stems to ground. Head back new growth. |
| *Artemisia* species, sagebrush, southernwood | ES, DS | control growth | late winter | Thin branches. Can cut back severely. |
| *Atriplex* species, saltbush | ES, DS | little pruning needed | anytime | Can shear into hedge. |
| *Aucuba japonica,* aucuba | ES | control growth | late spring–summer | Cut to pair of buds, leaf or branch. |
| Avocado | FT | develop framework | after fruiting | Train young tree for shape. Remove deadwood. |
| *Azara* species, azara | ES | shape | anytime | Pinch or head branches to shape. Can be trained as small tree or espalier. |

| Botanical name, common name | Plant Type | Pruning Goal | When to Prune | How to Prune |
|---|---|---|---|---|
| *Baccharis pilularis,* coyote brush | ES | little pruning needed | late winter | Thin old and dead wood. Head branches to shape. |
| Bamboo, includes many genera | G | control growth | during active growth | Remove old and dead stems each year. Cut out invasive growth. |
| *Beaumontia grandiflora,* herald's-trumpet | V | control growth | after flowering | Cut back lightly if overgrown. |
| *Berberis* species, barberry | ES, DS | thin, open up | late winter | Cut out old branches. Can be sheared into hedge. |
| *Betula* species, birch | BT | correct V-branching | late summer–winter | Cut off one branch in Vs. Remove deadwood. |
| *Bignonia capreolata,* trumpet flower | V | control growth | late winter | Remove tangles and dead or weak wood. |
| Blackberry | V | encourage fruiting | late winter, summer | See pages 48–49. |
| Blueberry | DS | encourage fruiting | late winter | See pages 46–47. |
| *Bougainvillea* species, bougainvillea | V | control growth | spring–autumn | Thin and head back as desired. |
| *Bouvardia longiflora* | ES | shape | early spring | Head flowering stems; pinch new growth. |
| *Brachychiton* species, bottle tree | FLT | early training | after flowering | Create framework; then little pruning needed. |
| *Brachysema lanceolatum,* scimitar shrub | ES | remove deadwood | early spring | Cut out deadwood. No other pruning needed. |
| *Breynia disticha,* snowbush | ES | shape | anytime | Head branches and pinch new growth to shape. |
| *Brugmansia* species, angel's-trumpet | ES | control growth | early spring | Head and pinch. Remove deadwood. |
| *Brunfelsia pauciflora calycina,* yesterday-today-and-tomorrow | ES | shape | spring or summer | Head and pinch to keep compact. |
| *Buddleia alternifolia,* fountain butterfly bush | FLT, DS | encourage new growth | after flowering | Cut out old wood. Thin and trim branches. |
| *Buddleia davidii,* common butterfly bush | DS, PES | encourage new growth | late winter | Cut out old wood. Head branches back. |
| *Buxus* species, boxwood | ES | shape | early spring–fall | Trim and shape as desired—freeform or hedge. |
| *Calliandra* species, powderpuff | ES | encourage new growth | after flowering | Remove oldest stems. Easy to espalier. |
| *Callicarpa* species, beautyberry | DS | encourage new growth | late winter | Cut entire plant or 2-year-old stems to ground. |
| *Callistemon* species, bottlebrush | FLT, ES | shape and fullness | spring or summer | Trim to side branches or buds. |
| *Calluna vulgaris,* Scotch heather | ES | tidy, compact shape | late summer–spring | Shear off dead flowers. Pinch in early spring. |
| *Calocedrus decurrens,* incense cedar | NT | shape as desired | early spring | Grow naturally or shear into hedge. |
| *Calycanthus* species, sweet shrub | DS | open, arching shape | early spring | Thin out old and dense growth. |
| *Camellia* species, camellia | ES | shape | after flowering | Thin old growth; pinch for fullness. |
| *Campsis* species, trumpet creeper | V | control growth | early spring | Head long branches; pinch for fullness. |
| *Cantua buxifolia,* magic flower | ES | open, arching shape | after flowering | Head and thin growth to direct shape. |
| *Caragana arborescens,* Siberian pea tree | DS | tidiness, shape | early spring | Remove faded flowers, deadwood and leggy growth. |
| *Carissa grandiflora,* natal plum | ES | shape | spring | Remove deadwood and overlong shoots. |
| *Carpenteria californica,* tree anemone | ES | shape, control size | after flowering | Prune to pair of leaves or branches. |
| *Carpinus* species, hornbeam | BT | good branch structure | late winter | Select strong laterals. Remove deadwood. |
| *Caryopteris* species, bluebeard | DS | encourage new growth | late winter | Cut back to ground. |
| *Casimiroa edulis,* white sapote | FT | control growth | spring | Thin and head back to desired size. |
| *Cassia* species, senna | FLT, PET, ES, PES | shape | after flowering | Some need light pruning. Prune fast-growing species more heavily. |
| *Castanea* species, chestnut | FT | good branch structure | late winter | Select strong laterals. Remove deadwood. |
| *Casuarina* species, she oak, beefwood | NT | good branch structure | anytime | Select strong laterals. Remove deadwood. |
| *Catalpa* species, catalpa | BT | good branch structure | late winter | Select strong laterals. Remove deadwood. |
| *Ceanothus americanus* and hybrids, New Jersey tea | BT, ES | shape | late winter | Thin and pinch to shape. |
| *Ceanothus* species, wild lilac | ES | shape | after flowering | Thin and pinch to shape; avoid large cuts. |

**67**

| Botanical name, common name | Plant Type | Pruning Goal | When to Prune | How to Prune |
|---|---|---|---|---|
| *Cedrus* species, cedar | NT | keep tidy | late summer–winter | Remove deadwood. See pages 24–25. |
| *Celastrus* species, bittersweet | V | control growth | late winter | Thin out old, weak stems. Cut others back by 1/3. |
| *Celtis* species, hackberry | BT | good branch structure | anytime but spring | Select strong laterals. Remove deadwood. |
| *Cephalanthus occidentalis*, buttonbush | DS | shape | early spring | Thin to open up and shape. Remove dead wood. |
| *Cephalotaxus* species, plum yew | NT, ES | little pruning needed | summer–winter | Pinch or trim to shape. |
| *Ceratonia siliqua*, carob | BT, ES | good branch structure | late winter | When young, thin and trim to shape. |
| *Cercidiphyllum japonicum*, katsura tree | BT, DS | shape | fall–early spring | Thin out and remove deadwood. |
| *Cercidium* species, palo verde | DT | little pruning needed | late spring–winter | Trim to clean up or shape. |
| *Cercis* species, redbud | FLT, DS | open up, shape | late winter | Thin and remove dead or crossing branches. |
| *Cercocarpus* species, mountain mahogany | BT, ES, DS | open up, shape | early spring | Remove deadwood. Thin to open up. |
| *Cestrum* species, cestrum | ES | clean up, control size | after flowering | Remove deadwood. Prune heavily to rejuvenate, if needed. |
| *Chaenomeles* species, flowering quince | DS | open up, control size | after flowering | If overgrown, remove up to 1/3 of old branches. |
| *Chamaecyparis* species, false cypress | NT, ES | little pruning needed | late summer–winter | See pages 24–25. |
| Cherry | FT | good branch structure | late winter | See pages 50–51. |
| *Chilopsis linearis*, desert willow | FLT, DS | shape | winter | Thin for pleasing shape. |
| *Chimonanthus praecox*, wintersweet | DS | encourage flowers | after flowering | Cut out weak wood. Thin for pleasing shape. |
| *Chionanthus* species, fringe tree | FLT | shape | after flowering | Prune into tree or shrub as desired. |
| *Choisya ternata*, Mexican orange | ES | fullness | summer | Thin old branches, pinch tips. |
| *Cinnamomum camphora*, camphor tree | BT | good branch structure | summer | Select strong laterals. Remove deadwood. |
| *Cistus* species, rock rose | ES | fullness, tidiness | after flowering | Pinch tips, remove deadwood. |
| Citrus | FT | little pruning needed | spring–fall | Thin as needed. Remove deadwood. |
| *Cladrastis lutea*, yellowwood | FLT | good branch structure | summer | Remove 1 limb in V-shaped crotches. |
| *Clematis* (spring-flowering) | V | keep tidy, control size | after flowering | See pages 38–39. |
| *Clematis* (summer-flowering) | V | keep tidy, control size | late winter | See pages 38–39. |
| *Clematis* (twice-flowering) | V | keep tidy, control size | late winter and early summer | See pages 38–39. |
| *Clerodendrum bungei*, kashmir-bouquet | ES | keep compact | early spring | Cut back heavily. Then pinch new growth. |
| *Clethra* species, summer-sweet | BT, DS | shape | early spring | Trim shrubs. Select good scaffolds on tree types. |
| *Clianthus puniceus*, glory pea | V | encourage new growth | after flowering | Cut out oldest wood. |
| *Clytostoma callistegioides*, violet trumpet vine | V | control growth | late winter–summer | Cut back to desired size. |
| *Coccoloba uvifera*, sea grape | BT, ES | shape | late spring–fall | Cut to create tree or shrub as desired. |
| *Cocculus* species, snailseed | BT, ES | arching shape | anytime | Thin to side branches; don't pinch. |
| *Coleonema* species, breath of heaven | ES | fullness | after flowering | Thin old stems. Shear lightly. |
| *Colutea arborescens*, bladder senna | ES | control size | summer | Cut back heavily. |
| *Convolvulus cneorum*, bush morning glory, silverbush | ES | control size, shape | late winter | Pinch or head back. Remove oldest stems. |
| *Coprosma* species, coprosma | ES | control size, shape | anytime | Head back as needed. |
| *Cornus* species, dogwood | DS | encourage new wood | late winter | Cut to ground or cut out old stems and head back others. |
| *Cornus* species, dogwood | FLT | train as tree or shrub little pruning needed | after flowering | Prune for desired shape. Remove deadwood. |
| *Corokia cotoneaster* | ES | shape | anytime | Cut out vertical branches. Little else to do. |
| *Correa* species, Australian fuchsia | ES | shape, fullness | after flowering | Cut to a leaf—never bare wood. Pinch new growth. |
| *Corylopsis* species, winter hazel | DS | little pruning needed | after flowering | Cut out deadwood. |

68

| Botanical name, common name | Plant Type | Pruning Goal | When to Prune | How to Prune |
|---|---|---|---|---|
| *Corylus* species, filbert, hazelnut | FT, DS | shape | late winter | Remove suckers. Train as tree or shrub. |
| *Corynocarpus laevigata,* New Zealand laurel | BT, ES | little pruning needed | anytime | Prune to desired shape. |
| *Cotinus coggygria,* smoke tree | FLT | tidiness | late winter | Remove deadwood. Train as tree or shrub. |
| *Cotoneaster* species, cotoneaster | ES, PES, DS | tidiness | late winter | Remove deadwood and wayward limbs. |
| *Crataegus* species, hawthorn | FLT, FT | tidiness | late winter | Remove deadwood and wayward limbs. |
| *Cryptomeria japonica,* Japanese cedar | NT | little pruning needed | anytime but spring | Remove deadwood and wayward limbs. |
| *Cunninghamia lanceolata,* China fir | NT | shape, tidiness | late winter | Remove deadwood and suckers. |
| *Cupressocyparis leylandii,* leyland cypress | NT | control size | anytime | Trim to desired height and width. |
| *Cupressus* species, cypress | NT | tidiness | anytime | Trim to shape; don't tie columnar types. |
| Currant | DS | encourage fruiting | late winter | See pages 46–47. |
| *Cytisus, Genista, Spartium* species, broom | ES, DS | shape, fullness | after flowering | Head back stems. Remove deadwood. |
| *Daboecia* species, Irish heath | ES | fullness, tidiness | early spring | Cut back by 1/2. Remove spent blooms. |
| *Daphne* species, daphne | ES, DS | shape | after flowering | Thin and head to create desired shape. |
| *Davidia involucrata,* dove tree | FLT | good branch structure | after flowering | Select strong laterals. Remove deadwood. |
| *Delonix regia,* royal poinciana | FLT | good branch structure | anytime | Select strong laterals. Remove deadwood. |
| *Dendromecon* species, bush poppy | ES | tidiness, fullness | after flowering | Cut out deadwood. Head back growth. |
| *Deutzia* species, deutzia | DS | encourage flowers | as flowers fade | Cut below flowers. Remove oldest stems. |
| *Diospyros* species, persimmon | FT | good branch structure | late winter | Select wide-angled scaffolds. |
| *Diplacus* species, monkeyflower | ES | shape | early spring–summer | Pinch new growth. Trim again after flowering. |
| *Distictis* species, trumpet vine | V | control growth | late fall–spring | Remove tangles; can head back severely. |
| *Dodonaea viscosa,* hopbush | ES | control growth | any time | Train as shrub or small tree. |
| *Dombeya* species | ES | shape | early spring | Train as shrubs, trees, espaliers or on arbors. |
| *Drimys winteri,* winter's-bark | FLT | little pruning needed | anytime | Trim to enhance shape. |
| *Duranta* species, golden-dewdrop | ES | shape | anytime | Thin and head back. Can train as small tree. |
| *Echium fastuosum,* pride of Madeira | ES | fullness | after flowering | Cut faded flower spikes to foliage. Never cut into bare wood. |
| *Elaeagnus* species, Russian olive, silver berry | BT, ES, DS | shape | early summer | Clip off wayward branches. |
| *Enkianthus* species | DS | little pruning needed | late winter | Cut out dead or damaged wood. |
| *Eranthemum pulchellum,* blue sage | ES | fullness, flowers | spring | Pinch tips. Renew plant by cutting to ground. |
| *Erica* species, heath | ES | fullness | after flowering | Shear flowering stems back to leafy growth, never bare stems. |
| *Eriobotrya japonica,* loquat | FLT, FT | shape | late winter | Train as shrub, tree, espalier. Thin fruit. |
| *Eriogonum* species, wild buckwheat | ES | fullness | spring | Pinch tips of new growth. |
| *Erythrina* species, coral tree | FLT | shape | winter | Select strong laterals. Remove deadwood. |
| *Erythrina herbacea,* coral bean | ES | shape | late winter | Prune to shape. Can cut to ground. |
| *Escallonia* species, escallonia | ES | shape, openness | late winter | Thin out old wood. Head wayward branches. |
| *Eucalyptus* species, gum tree | BT, ES | tidiness, control size | spring–summer | Remove deadwood. Eliminate narrow Vs. Can cut back severely. |
| *Euonymus japonica,* Japanese spindle tree | BT, ES | shape | late winter | Cut out deadwood, errant branches. Can shear. |
| *Euonymus* species, spindle tree, burning bush | DS | shape, openness | late winter | Remove 1/3 oldest stems and errant branches. |
| *Euonymus fortunei,* euonymus | V | control growth | early spring–summer | Trim several times. Can be cut to ground. |
| *Euphorbia pulcherimma,* poinsettia | ES, DS | encourage flowers | after flowering | Prune to shape. Can cut back severely. |

| Botanical name, common name | Plant Type | Pruning Goal | When to Prune | How to Prune |
|---|---|---|---|---|
| *Eurya* species | ES | little pruning needed | late spring | Cut to side branch or bud. |
| *Euryops* species, euryops | ES | fullness, shape | summer | Pinch new growth. Cut wayward stems to a leaf. |
| *Exochorda* species, pearl bush | DS | tall, arching shape | after flowering | Cut old and weak wood to ground. |
| *Fagus* species, beech | BT | good branch structure | late winter | Select strong laterals. Remove deadwood. |
| *Fallugia paradoxa,* Apache-plume | PES | little pruning needed | fall | Cut back to a leaf or bud. |
| *Fatshedera lizei* | ES, V | fullness, control size | anytime | Pinch tips. Prune as needed. Can cut to ground. |
| *Fatsia japonica,* Japanese aralia | ES | shape, control size | early spring | Hard to hurt this plant–prune as desired. |
| *Feijoa sellowiana,* pineapple guava | FLT, FT, ES | shape | spring | Can train as tree, espalier or shrub. |
| *Felicia amelloides,* blue marguerite | ES | tidiness, fullness | late summer | Shear, but not into bare, woody growth. |
| *Ficus* species, ornamental fig | BT, ES, DS | shape | spring | Train as shrub or tree. Pinch to shape. Head overlong branches. Thin annually. |
| *Ficus repens,* creeping fig | V | control size | spring | Cut to ground every few years. |
| Fig | FT | low, open shape | late winter | Cut out limbs to shape and create open center. |
| *Forsythia* species, golden bells | DS | encourage flowers | after flowering | Cut out deadwood, 1/3 oldest stems. Pinch tips. |
| *Fothergilla* species | DS | little pruning needed | late winter | Occasionally cut out old, weak or deadwood. |
| *Franklinia alatamaha,* Franklin tree | FLT | shape | early spring | Train as single or multitrunked tree. |
| *Fraxinus* species, ash | BT | good branch structure | late winter | Prune when young to eliminate narrow V-crotches. |
| *Fremontodendron* species, fremontia | FLT, ES | shape, control size | after flowering | Pinch tips, head wayward branches. |
| *Fuchsia* species, fuchsia | ES, DS | promote flowering | winter and spring | Heavy pruning in winter. Pinch in spring. |
| *Gardenia* species, gardenia | ES | fullness, shape | while blooming | Pinch out weak or overlong branches. |
| *Garrya elliptica,* silk-tassel | ES | shape | after flowering | Cut to lateral branch or pair of leaves. |
| *Gaultheria* species | ES | tidiness | spring | Cut out dead or old branches. |
| *Geijera parviflora,* Australian willow | BT | good branch structure | any time | Cut out deadwood. Allow weeping habit. |
| *Ginkgo biloba,* maidenhair tree | BT | good branch structure | late winter | Cut out vertical shoots, poorly placed limbs. |
| *Gleditsia triacanthos,* honey locust | BT | good branch structure | late winter | Eliminate narrow V-shaped crotches and vertical shoots. |
| Grape | V | encourage fruit | winter and summer | See pages 54–57. |
| *Grevillea robusta,* silk oak | FLT | good branch structure | after flowering | Thin and head back overlong limbs. |
| *Grevillea* species, grevillea | ES | little pruning needed | anytime | Pinch to shape. |
| *Grewia occidentalis,* lavender starflower | ES | flowers, bushiness | late spring, fall | Pinch lightly after bloom. Prune in fall. Can be sheared. |
| *Griselinia* species | ES | bushiness | early spring | Prune wayward limbs to a lateral, leaf or bud. |
| *Gymnocladus dioica,* Kentucky coffee tree | BT | good branch structure | late winter | Select strong laterals. Cut out deadwood. |
| *Hakea* species, hakea | FLT, ES | shape, bushiness | early spring | Pinch tips on young plants for fullness. |
| *Halesia* species, silver-bell | FLT | shape | after flowering | Train as tree or multistemmed shrub. |
| *Hamamelis* species, witch hazel | FLT, DS | shape, open up | after flowering | Cut out old, weak or dead stems. Pinch. |
| *Hardenbergia* species | V | shape, control size | after flowering | Remove tangles, old stems. Pinch back. |
| *Harpephyllum caffrum,* Kaffir plum | FLT | good branch structure | early spring | Select strong laterals. Thin. Remove deadwood. |
| *Hebe* species, hebe | ES | bushiness, control size | after flowering | Cut out old limbs, head back stems. |
| *Hedera* species, ivy | V | control size | anytime | Trim several times a year. Can cut to ground. |
| *Heteromeles arbutifolia,* toyon | FLT, ES | shape | late winter | Train as shrub or small tree. |
| *Hibiscus rosa-sinensis,* Chinese hibiscus | ES | flowers, bushiness | spring | Pinch new growth. Thin out old branches. |
| *Hibiscus syriacus,* rose-of-Sharon | DS | shape | winter | Thin, remove deadwood. Head long stems. |

| Botanical name, common name | Plant Type | Pruning Goal | When to Prune | How to Prune |
|---|---|---|---|---|
| *Holodiscus* species | DS | tidiness | after flowering | Cut off old blooms, long laterals and deadwood. |
| *Hydrangea* species | DS, V | shape, flowers | late winter | Cut back stems. Cut out dead, weak wood. |
| *Hydrangea macrophylla,* bigleaf hydrangea | DS | shape, flowers | after flowering; late winter in cold climates | Cut back stems. Cut out dead, weak wood. |
| *Hymenosporum flavum,* sweetshade | FLT | good branch structure | anytime | Pinch tips of new growth regularly. |
| *Hypericum* species, St.-Johns-wort | ES, PES | fullness | late winter | Cut back heavily every 3 years. |
| *Ilex* species, holly | BT, ES, DS | shape | winter | Cut at Christmas and use as trim. |
| *Illicium* species, anise tree | FLT | little pruning needed | spring | Cut wayward branches. |
| *Itea virginica,* Virginia sweetspire | FLT, ES | shape | early spring | Cut out deadwood, thin out old stems. |
| *Ixora coccinea,* flame-of-the-woods | ES | bushiness | early spring–fall | Pinch young stems, cut out old ones. |
| *Jacaranda mimosifolia,* jacaranda | FLT | good branch structure | spring | Train to single or multitrunked tree. |
| *Jasminum* species, jasmine | ES, DS, V | shape, control growth | after flowering | Prune to desired shape or size. |
| *Juniperus* species, juniper | NT, ES | shape, open up | spring–summer | See pages 26–27. |
| *Kalmia latifolia,* mountain laurel | ES | little pruning needed | after flowering | Remove faded flowers. Pinch terminal buds to shape. |
| *Kerria japonica,* kerria | DS | encourage flowers | after flowering | Cut out most stems that flowered. |
| *Koelreuteria* species, goldenrain tree | FLT | good branch structure | late winter | Select strong laterals. Remove deadwood. |
| *Kolkwitzia amabilis,* beautybush | DS | encourage flowers | after flowering | Thin out old and deadwood. |
| *Laburnum* species, goldenchain tree | FLT | good branch structure | after flowering | Select strong laterals. Cut off seed pods. |
| *Lagerstroemia indica,* crape myrtle | FLT, DS | train as shrub or tree | late winter | Prune for shape. Trim all growth each year. |
| *Lantana* species | ES, DS | tidiness | spring | Cut back as much as needed. Cut out deadwood. |
| *Lapageria rosea,* Chilean bellflower | V | tidiness | early spring | Cut out tangles and deadwood. |
| *Larix* species, larch | NT | little pruning needed | late winter | Cut out dead or damaged wood. |
| *Laurus nobilis,* sweet bay | BT, ES | shape, topiary | spring–summer | Responds well to pruning but little needed. |
| *Lavandula* species, lavender | ES | bushiness | early spring | Shear or trim back (after flowering in cold climates). |
| *Leptospermum* species, tea tree | FLT, ES | little pruning needed | after flowering | Cut into leafy area, not to bare wood. |
| *Leucophyllum frutescens,* Texas ranger | ES | shape | late winter | Trim long branches, cut out deadwood. |
| *Leucothoe* species | ES | arching form | after flowering | Prune out old branches. Pinch new growth. |
| *Ligustrum* species, privet | BT, ES, DS | shape | late winter–summer | Grow naturally or prune as hedge or topiary. |
| *Lindera benzoin,* spicebush | DS | tidiness | after flowering | Cut out a few old branches each year. |
| *Liquidambar styraciflua,* sweet gum | BT | little pruning needed | late winter | Do not prune for first 4 years. Thin as needed. |
| *Liriodendron tulipifera,* tulip tree | BT | little pruning needed | summer | Cut out very upright branches. |
| *Litchi chinensis,* litchi nut | FT | train and shape | summer | Prune as single or multitrunked tree. |
| *Lithocarpus densiflorus,* tanbark oak | BT | little pruning needed | early spring | Remove deadwood. |
| *Lonicera* species, honeysuckle | ES, DS | shape | late winter | Cut out old stems and deadwood. Can shear. |
| *Lonicera fragrantissima,* winter honeysuckle | PES, DS | shape | after flowering | Cut out old stems and deadwood. Can shear. |
| *Lonicera* species, honeysuckle | V | control size | after flowering | Cut back heavily. Thin older growth. |
| *Loropetalum chinense* | ES | little pruning needed | after spring flowers | Cut out dead or damaged wood. |
| *Lyonothamnus floribundus,* Catalina ironwood | FLT | good branch structure | winter | Cut out water sprouts, head overlong limbs. |
| *Lysiloma thornberi,* feather bush | BT, ES, DS | shape | spring | Thin. Remove deadwood. Can train to single trunk. |
| *Macfadyena unguis-cati,* cat's-claw | V | control size | after flowering | Cut out old stems, weak growth. Pinch tips. |
| *Maclura pomifera,* osage orange | BT | shape | winter | Train as single or multitrunked. |

| Botanical name, common name | Plant Type | Pruning Goal | When to Prune | How to Prune |
|---|---|---|---|---|
| *Magnolia* species, magnolia | FLT | little pruning needed | summer | Shape when young. Large cuts heal slowly. |
| *Mahonia* species, holly grape | ES | tidiness | after flowering | Cut out old stems, trim to shape. |
| *Malus* species, crab apple | FLT, FT | keep framework open | after flowering | Cut out crossing branches, deadwood. |
| *Malvaviscus arboreus*, Turk's-cap | ES, V | tidiness | spring–autumn | Thin and trim. Cut out oldest stems. |
| *Mandevilla laxa*, Chilean jasmine | V | control size | late winter | Cut out tangles. Can cut to ground. |
| *Maytenus boaria*, mayten tree | BT | little pruning needed | spring | Train as single or multitrunked tree. |
| *Melaleuca* species, bottlebrush | FLT, ES | shape | anytime | Cut to side branches, never bare wood. |
| *Melia azedarach*, Chinaberry | FLT | good branch structure | late winter | Select strong laterals. Cut out deadwood. |
| *Melianthus major*, honeybush | ES | tidiness, shape | early spring | Remove old or lanky stems. |
| *Metasequoia glyptostroboides*, dawn redwood | NT | little pruning needed | late winter | Cut overlong limbs to lateral growth. |
| *Michelia doltsopa* | FT, ES | shape | spring | Grow naturally. Can train as single trunked tree. |
| *Michelia figo*, banana shrub | ES | shape | spring | Grow naturally. Can shear or topiary. |
| *Morus* species, mulberry | BT | good branch structure | late winter | Head overlong branches, cut out deadwood. |
| *Muehlenbeckia* species, wire vine | V | control growth | anytime | Cut back or shear as needed. |
| *Murraya paniculata*, orange jessamine | ES | shape | early spring | Cut overlong branches to shape. |
| *Myoporum* species, myoporum | BT, ES | shape | spring | Trim wayward branches. |
| *Myrica* species, wax myrtle | ES, DS | little pruning needed | late winter | Cut out old stems occasionally. |
| *Myrsine africana*, African boxwood | ES | shape | anytime | Pinch or trim to shape. Can shear. |
| *Myrtus communis*, myrtle | ES | shape | anytime | Trim or thin to shape. Can shear. |
| *Nandina domestica*, heavenly bamboo | ES | bushiness | late winter | Cut out old stems occasionally. |
| Nectarine | FT | encourage fruit | late winter | See pages 58–59. |
| *Nerium oleander*, oleander | ES | shape, control size | early spring | Cut out old stems, trim back. |
| *Nyssa sylvatica*, tupelo, sour gum | BT | good branch structure | late winter | Cut out weak limbs, deadwood. |
| *Ochna serrulata*, Mickey-Mouse plant | ES | little pruning needed | early spring | Pinch long branches to encourage bushiness. |
| *Oemleria cerasiformis*, osoberry | DS | bushiness | late winter | Cut out old stems. Can train as tree. |
| *Olea europaea*, olive | BT | shape | early spring | Train as tree or shrub. Pull off water sprouts. |
| *Olmediella betschlerana*, Costa Rican holly | BT, ES | shape | early spring | Train as tree or shrub. |
| *Osmanthus* species, sweet olive, | BT, ES | shape | spring–summer | Cut back overlong stems; pinch for fullness. |
| *Ostrya* species, hop hornbeam | BT | good branch structure | late winter | Select strong scaffolds. Can allow several trunks. |
| *Oxera pulchella*, royal climber | V | shape | after flowering | Trim as desired. Can train as vine. |
| *Oxydendrum arboreum*, sourwood | FLT | good branch structure | late winter | Select strong scaffolds. Can allow several trunks. |
| *Paeonia suffruticosa* hybrids, tree peony | PS | little pruning needed | early spring | Cut out deadwood. Cut off faded blooms. |
| Palm, includes many genera | BT | tidiness | anytime | Cut off dead fronds occasionally. |
| *Pandorea* species | V | shape, control size | anytime | Cut out tangles, dead stems. Head back after bloom. |
| *Parkinsonia aculeata*, Mexican palo verde | FLT | good branch structure | anytime | Select good scaffolds, cut out deadwood. |
| *Parrotia persica* | BT | little pruning needed | late winter | Can train to single trunked tree. |
| *Parthenocissus* species, Boston ivy, Virginia creeper | V | control size | winter and spring | Head back in winter. Occasionally cut to ground. |
| *Passiflora* species, passionflower vine | V | control size | spring–fall | Cut out tangles, overlong stems, deadwood. |
| *Paulownia tomentosa*, Princess tree | FLT | good branch structure | late winter | Head back overlong branches on young trees. |
| *Paxistima* species | ES | little pruning needed | anytime | Can shear into hedge. |

| Botanical name, common name | Plant Type | Pruning Goal | When to Prune | How to Prune |
|---|---|---|---|---|
| Peach | FT | encourage fruiting | late winter | See pages 58–59. |
| Pear | FT | encourage fruiting | late winter | See pages 60–61. |
| Pecan | FT | good branch structure | after nuts drop | See pages 64–65. |
| *Pernettya mucronata*, pernettya | ES | tidiness | early spring | Cut out old stems, deadwood. Trim long stems. |
| *Philadelphus* species, mock orange | DS | encourage flowers | after flowering | Cut out old stems, cut new ones to side shoots. |
| *Phillyrea decora* | ES | little pruning needed | early spring | Cut overlong stems back to a pair of leaves. |
| *Phlomis fruticosa*, Jerusalem sage | ES | control size, shape | autumn | Cut out weak stems, cut others back. |
| *Photinia* species, photinia | ES, DS | control size, shape | late winter | Cut out old stems, trim others back to shape. |
| *Physocarpus* species, ninebark | DS | little pruning needed | late winter | Cut out old stems, pinch shoots for fullness. |
| *Picea* species, spruce | NT | little pruning needed | late winter or spring | See pages 24–25. |
| *Pieris* species, pieris | ES | little pruning needed | after flowering | Cut back to control size. Remove faded flowers. |
| *Pinus* species, pine | NT | little pruning needed | late winter or spring | See pages 24–25. |
| *Pistacia* species, pistachio | BT, FT | good branch structure | late winter | Select strong scaffolds. |
| *Pittosporum* species, pittosporum | BT | good branch structure | anytime | Train to single or multitrunks. |
| *Pittosporum* species, pittosporum | ES | shape | anytime | Cut overlong stems to side branches. |
| *Platanus* species, plane tree | BT | good branch structure | late winter | Select strong leader and lateral limbs. |
| *Platycladus orientalis*, oriental arborvitae | NT, ES | little pruning needed | late winter | Cut wayward limbs to foliage, never bare wood. |
| Plum | FT | encourage fruiting | late winter | See pages 62–63. |
| *Plumbago auriculata*, Cape leadwort | PES, V | shape | late winter | Trim back wayward branches. Can be cut to ground. |
| *Podocarpus* species, yew pine, fern pine | BT, ES | little pruning needed | spring–summer | Train to shrub or single or multitrunked tree. Trim to shape. Can shear to hedge. |
| *Polygala dalmaisiana*, sweet-pea shrub | ES | bushiness | anytime | Shear or trim back several times each year. |
| *Polygonum* species, knotweed | V | tidiness, shape | early spring | Cut out deadwood, head back stems. Can cut to ground. |
| *Poncirus trifoliata*, hardy orange | ES | good branch structure | late winter | Cut out weak, deadwood. Thin canopy. |
| *Populus* species, poplar, cottonwood, aspen | BT | little pruning needed | late winter | Cut out dead, weak wood. |
| *Potentilla fruticosa*, cinquefoil | DS | tidiness, bushiness | winter and after bloom | Cut out deadwood. After bloom, thin and trim. |
| *Prosopis* species, mesquite | BT, ES, DS | tidiness | winter | Cut out deadwood, thin dense growth. |
| Prune | FT | encourage fruit | late winter | See pages 62–63. |
| *Prunus* species | BT, ES | shape | anytime | Cut out deadwood, head back overlong limbs. |
| *Prunus* species, flowering almond | FLT | encourage flowers | after flowering | Cut out deadwood. Thin to encourage new wood. |
| *Prunus* species, flowering cherry | FLT | good branch structure | after flowering | Little trimming needed after shape is established. |
| *Prunus* species, flowering peach, nectarine | FLT | encourage new growth | after flowering | Cut out old, deadwood; thin rest. Head stems back. |
| *Prunus* species, flowering plum | FLT | good branch structure | after flowering | Cut out upright and crossing limbs. |
| *Pseudolarix kaempferi*, golden larch | NT | establish straight trunk | late winter | Once trunk established, little pruning needed. |
| *Pseudopanax arboreum*, five-fingers | BT, ES | little pruning needed | spring | Train as single or multitrunked tree. |
| *Pseudotsuga menziesii*, Douglas fir | NT | good branch structure | early summer | Train to straight, single leader. Can prune into hedge. |
| *Pterocarya stenoptera*, Chinese wingnut | BT | good branch structure | late winter | Cut out deadwood at lateral growth. |
| *Pterostyrax hispidus*, epaulette tree | FLT | good branch structure | late winter | Can grow as multitrunked tree. |
| *Punica granatum*, pomegranate | FLT, FT | control growth, shape | winter | Grow as single or multitrunked tree. Thin heavily. |

| Botanical name, common name | Plant Type | Pruning Goal | When to Prune | How to Prune |
|---|---|---|---|---|
| *Pyracantha* species, fire thorn | ES | shape | late winter | Can prune heavily.<br>Natural shape is good. |
| *Pyrostegia venusta,* flame vine | V | control growth | late winter | Can cut back heavily. Remove tangles. |
| *Pyrus* species, ornamental pear | FLT | good branch structure | late winter | Train trunk, head back overlong stems. |
| *Quercus* species, oak | BT | good branch structure | late winter or summer | Thin; make cuts to side branches. |
| *Quillaja saponaria,* soap-bark tree | BT | single or multitrunk | anytime | Once established, just cut out deadwood. |
| Quince, fruiting | FT | train as tree or shrub | late winter | Thin to side branches, shape long growth. |
| *Raphiolepis* species, India or Yedda hawthorn | ES | shape | after flowering | Thin old growth, head back long stems to shape. |
| Raspberry | V | encourage fruiting | varies with type | See pages 48–49. |
| *Rhamnus* species | BT, ES, DS | little pruning needed | anytime | Pinch to shape. Shear hedges in late winter. |
| *Rhododendron* species, azalea | ES, DS | shape | early spring | Pinch anywhere to shape. Can shear. |
| *Rhododendron* species, rhododendron | ES, DS | shape, fullness | early spring | Remove faded flowers. Cut leggy limbs to leaf whorl. |
| *Rhodotypos scandens,* jetbead | DS | fullness | late winter | Cut out oldest stems, pinch shoots. |
| *Rhoicissus capensis,* evergreen grape | V | control growth, shape | spring | Pinch tips, thin if overgrown. |
| *Rhus* species, sumac | DS | little pruning needed | winter or summer | Remove deadwood. |
| *Rhus* species, sumac | BT, ES | train as tree or shrub | early spring | Can hedge or espalier. Shape as desired. |
| *Ribes* species, flowering currant & gooseberry | ES, DS | shape, tidiness | after flowering | Cut out oldest and deadwood; don't leave stubs. |
| *Robinia* species, locust | BT, DS | good branch structure | late winter | Once shape established, cut out deadwood. |
| *Rondeletia* species | ES | bushiness | after flowering | Cut back and pinch new growth. |
| *Rosa* species and hybrids, rose | DS | shape, flowers | varies | See pages 32–36. |
| *Rosmarinus officinalis,* rosemary | ES | control growth | after flowering | Head back into leafy wood only.<br>Pinch new growth. |
| *Rubus deliciosus,* Rocky Mountain thimbleberry | DS | encourage flowers | fall or winter | Cut stems that flowered to the ground. |
| *Salix* species, willow | BT | strong central leader | late winter | Cut out water sprouts, deadwood. |
| *Salix* species, willow | DS | control density | early spring | Cut out oldest stems. Can cut to ground. |
| *Sambucus* species, elderberry | BT, DS | single or multitrunk | late winter | Cut out deadwood and water sprouts.<br>Head back long stems. |
| *Santolina* species, lavender cotton | ES | bushiness, fullness | early spring | Head back yearly. Can shear into hedge<br>Trim after flowering. |
| *Sapium sebiferum,* Chinese tallow tree | BT | single or multitrunk | late winter | Prune to shape. Cut out deadwood. |
| *Sarcococca* species, sweet box | ES | shape | anytime | Head wayward stems. Can cut to ground. |
| *Sassafras albidum,* sassafras | BT | little pruning needed | late winter | Cut out deadwood, water sprouts. |
| *Schinus* species, pepper tree | BT | good branch structure | early spring | Train when young. Avoid large cuts. |
| *Sciadopitys verticillata,* umbrella pine | NT | develop single trunk | summer | Little pruning needed once trunk develops. |
| *Sequoia sempervirens,* coast redwood | NT | little pruning needed | early summer | If second leader grows, cut it off.<br>Remove suckers. |
| *Sequoiadendron giganteum,* giant sequoia | NT | little pruning needed | early summer | If second leader grows, cut it off. |
| *Sesbania tripetii,* scarlet wistaria tree | FLT, DS | single or multistem | early spring | Cut year-old stems back to buds. |
| *Severinia buxifolia,* Chinese box orange | ES | shear into hedge | spring | Prune as needed to maintain shape. |
| *Shepherdia* species, buffalo berry | DS | shape, tidiness | late winter | Cut out old stems to open up. |
| *Simmondsia chinensis,* jojoba | ES | little pruning needed | early spring | Can shear into hedge. |
| *Skimmia* species | ES | little pruning needed | late spring | Head wayward stems. |
| *Solandra maxima,* cup-of-gold vine | V | bushiness | late spring | Cut back stems and pinch new growth. |
| *Solanum jasminoides,* potato vine | V | control growth | late winter–summer | Cut out tangles, head back.<br>Can prune severely. |
| *Sollya heterophylla,* Australian bluebell creeper | ES, V | control growth | spring | Cut out unwanted stems, trim back. |
| *Sophora japonica,* Japanese pagoda tree | FLT | good branch structure | late summer | Cut out weak, crossing branches when young. |

| Botanical name, common name | Plant Type | Pruning Goal | When to Prune | How to Prune |
|---|---|---|---|---|
| *Sorbaria* species, false spiraea | DS | flowers, control spread | late winter | Dig out spreading stems. Cut 1-year stems to 2 buds. |
| *Sorbus* species, mountain ash | BT | single or multitrunk | late winter | After shape established, thin center as needed. |
| *Sparmannia africana*, African linden | BT. ES | control growth | anytime | Thin oldest growth. Cut off faded flowers. |
| *Spathodea campanulata*, African tulip tree | FLT | good branch structure | spring or summer | Early training, then just cut out deadwood. |
| *Spiraea* species (spring blooming), spiraea | DS | arching shape | after flowering | Cut out oldest stems. |
| *Spiraea* species (summer blooming), spiraea | DS | large flowers | late winter | Cut back severely. Can cut to just 2 buds per stem. |
| *Stachyurus praecox* | DS | little pruning needed | after flowering | Thin and head back to lateral limbs. |
| *Stenocarpus sinuatus*, firewheel tree | FLT | good branch structure | spring | Cut out deadwood. |
| *Stewartia* species, stewartia | FLT, DS | single or multitrunk | late winter | Train as desired. Cut out deadwood. |
| *Stigmaphyllon* species, orchid vine | V | control growth | late winter | Cut out tangles, deadwood. Head back stems. |
| *Stranvaesia davidiana*, stranvaesia | ES | shape | late winter | Cut stems back to another branch. |
| *Streptosolen jamesonii*, marmalade bush | ES | flowers, shape | late winter | Cut out old, weak stems. After flowering, cut stems back. |
| *Styrax* species, snowbell | FLT, DS | shape, openness | after flowering | Cut out weak, thin, dead branches. Head long laterals. |
| *Symphoricarpos* species, snow & coralberry | DS | control growth | early spring | Cut 3-year-old growth to ground. |
| *Symplocos paniculata*, sapphire berry | DS | shape, control growth | early spring | Cut out old stems, head back overlong stems. |
| *Syringa vulgaris*, lilac | DS | shape, flowers | after flowering | See pages 28–29. |
| *Syzygium* species | FLT, ES | little pruning needed | late spring | Can shear into a hedge. |
| *Tabebuia* species, trumpet tree | FLT | good branch structure | after flowering | Establish structure, then trim as needed. |
| *Tamarix* species, spring-blooming tamarisk | FLT | open up | after flowering | Cut out old and weak, or crossing branches. |
| *Tamarix* species, summer-blooming tamarisk | FLT | control growth | late winter | Shape as trees or cut to ground for shrubs. |
| *Taxodium* species, cypress | NT | strong central leader | summer | Once leader is established, little pruning needed. |
| *Taxus* species, yew | NT | shape | winter–summer | Can leave alone or shape or shear as desired. |
| *Tecoma stans*, yellowbells | FLT, ES | shape, tidiness | late winter | Cut out deadwood. Can train as tree. |
| *Tecomaria capensis*, cape honeysuckle | V | control growth | after flowering | Trim and shape as desired. |
| *Ternstroemia gymnanthera* | ES | shape | late spring | Pinch new growth, head overlong stems. |
| *Tetrapanax papyriferus*, rice-paper plant | ES | shape | anytime | Thin stems for attractive shape. |
| *Teucrium* species, germander | ES | shape, fullness | late winter | Head back. Can shear into a hedge. |
| *Thevetia* species, yellow oleander | FLT, ES | shape, keep open | late winter | Cut out old stems, trim to shape. |
| *Thuja occidentalis*, American arborvitae | NT | shape | late winter | Shear to shape. Prune back to green growth. |
| *Thuja plicata*, Western red cedar | NT | little pruning needed | late winter | Natural shape best. Can be sheared. |
| *Tibouchina urvilleana*, princess flower | FLT, ES | shape, fullness | spring | Pinch new growth. Head back after bloom. |
| *Tilia* species, linden | BT | good branch structure | late winter | Cut out deadwood. |
| *Trachelospermum jasminoides*, star jasmine | V | shape, fullness | spring | Trim back overlong new growth. Pinch tips. |
| *Tsuga* species, hemlock | NT | shape | spring | Natural shape fine. Can shear to hedge. |
| *Turraea obtusifolia*, star bush | ES | little pruning needed | anytime | Can shear to hedge. |
| *Ugni molinae*, Chilean guava | ES | shape | anytime | Trim and head back to desired shape. |
| *Ulmus* species, elm | BT | good branch structure | late winter | Eliminate narrow V-crotches and crossing branches. |
| *Umbellularia californica*, California bay | BT | single or multitrunk | summer | Once established, trim to shape. |

| Botanical name, common name | Plant Type | Pruning Goal | When to Prune | How to Prune |
|---|---|---|---|---|
| *Vaccinium parvifolium*, red huckleberry | DS | little pruning needed | late winter | Cut out old, deadwood. |
| *Vaccinium* species, blueberry | ES, DS | encourage fruit | late winter | See pages 46–47. |
| *Vaccinium vitis-idaea*, cowberry | ES | control spread | summer | Dig out spreading stems at base. |
| *Viburnum* species, spring blooming | ES, DS | keep open, shape | after flowering | Cut out old or dead stems, head others. |
| *Viburnum* species, summer blooming | ES, DS | shape, keep open | late winter | Cut out old or dead stems, head others. |
| *Vitex agnus-castus*, chaste tree | FLT, DS | encourage flowers | late winter | Cut back heavily. |
| Walnut | FT | encourage nuts | summer or fall | See pages 64–65. |
| *Weigela* species | DS | new growth | after flowering | Cut out 2-year-old stems. Head others. |
| *Westringia rosmariniformis* | ES | little pruning needed | after first flowers | Head overlong stems to lateral growth. Can be sheared. |
| *Wisteria* species | V | control growth | late winter | See page 38. |
| *Xylosma congestum* | BT | little pruning needed | late winter | Can train as espalier, small tree. |
| *Yucca* species, yucca | ES | tidiness | after flowering | Cut off spent flower stalks. Cut out extra clumps. |
| *Zelkova serrata*, saw-leaf zelkova | BT | good branch structure | late winter | Can train as single or multitrunk. |
| *Zenobia pulverulenta*, dusty zenobia | DS | shape | late winter | Head back overlong stems. Cut out old stems periodically. |
| *Ziziyphus jujuba*, Chinese jujube | FLT, FT | strong central leader | late winter | Once leader established, thin out excess limbs. |

# INDEX

# A Note From
# NK Lawn & Garden Co.

For more than 100 years, since its founding in Minneapolis, Minnesota, NK Lawn & Garden has provided gardeners with the finest quality seed and other garden products.

We doubt that our leaders, Jesse E. Northrup and Preston King, would recognize their seed company today, but gardeners everywhere in the U.S. still rely on NK Lawn & Garden's knowledge and experience at planting time.

We are pleased to be able to share this practical experience with you through this ongoing series of easy-to-use gardening books.

Here you'll find hundreds of years of gardening experience distilled into easy-to-understand text and step-by-step pictures. Every popular gardening subject is included.

As you use the information in these books, we hope you'll also try our lawn and garden products. They're available at your local garden retailer.

There's nothing more satisfying than a successful, beautiful garden. There's something special about the color of blooming flowers and the flavor of home-grown garden vegetables.

We understand how special you feel about growing things—and NK Lawn & Garden feels the same way, too. After all, we've been a friend to gardeners everywhere since 1884.